# The Best Democracy Money Can Buy

*Reflections on Anti-Enlightenment and the Agony of Liberal Democracies*

Jorge Majfud

HUMANUS

SAN DIEGO-ACAPULCO

*The Best Democracy Money Can Buy: Reflections on Post-Enlightenment and the
Agony of Liberal Democracies*
© Jorge Majfud May 2025. jmajfud@ju.edu
© Humanus Editors 2025
ISBN: 978-1-956760-37-8
Humanus.info
editor@humanus.com / cuauhtemoceditorial@gmail.com

# TABLE OF CONTENTS

# DEMOCRACY AND CAPITALISM

# Native American Democracy

The new white democracy of the Thirteen Colonies, ostensibly founded on the Enlightenment ideas of radical philosophers, was far less democratic than the centuries-old confederation of Iroquois tribes. The League of Six Nations, Iroquois League, or Great League of Peace, had been established in 1142 through the integration of various Indigenous peoples of North America as a solution to a period of conflicts and individual power struggles. It was one of the oldest participatory democracies on the planet, based on the pursuit of peace and the redistribution of collective production.

The Iroquois accepted immigrants, displaced peoples, and even their defeated enemies in wars. Although some prisoners could be forced to labor, their servitude wasn't tied to race, and after some time, they were usually adopted by established families.

American Indigenous peoples practiced more democratic, less patriarchal (in many aspects matriarchal), and more equitable systems than Europeans. Examples of European democracy were limited to small groups, like in England's case, following the destruction of traditional communal lands and the commercialization of nearly everything at gunpoint—as seen with transnational companies and even pirates themselves, who established a hallmark of Western capitalism: pleasant democracies internally and upward; brutal dictatorships externally and downward.

In stark contrast to the new capitalist societies in Europe, in the Americas social success was reflected in higher life expectancy and greater average height than Europeans, due to better health and working conditions. Natives worked fewer hours per day—half as many days per year as European laborers. They had consolidated a social security system that protected the most vulnerable members, like the elderly and sick, exhibited much lower social inequality, and engaged in international wars far less frequently than Europeans.

A well-known example of democracy in North America, centuries before the founding of the so-called "American democracy," was the federation of Iroquois peoples, which founders like Benjamin Franklin knew well but deliberately omitted from voluminous constitutional and unionist debates. The reason isn't hard to guess, considering the chronic racism of the so-called Founding Fathers. Franklin himself, in a March 20, 1751 letter to James Parker arguing for the possibility of creating a federation of twelve independent colonies, referenced the shame that English colonists couldn't achieve what had long been accomplished by "six nations of ignorant savages." According to Franklin: *"It would be a very strange thing if six nations of ignorant savages should be capable of forming a scheme for such a union, and be able to execute it in such a manner as that it has subsisted ages and appears indissoluble; and yet that a like union should be impracticable for ten or a dozen English colonies, to whom it is more necessary, and must be more advantageous, and who cannot be supposed to want an equal understanding of their interests."* The thirteen arrows now held by the eagle on the U.S. shield originated from an Iroquois metaphor: it's easier to break many arrows separately than to break them all together.

Forty years later, shortly after the independence of the Thirteen Colonies and the expulsion of various Indigenous peoples beyond the Appalachians in 1784, Benjamin Franklin tempered his youthful judgments:

*"In their youth, Indians are hunters and warriors; when old, they become counselors, for all their governance rests on the counsel of the wise.*

*They have no force* [police], *no prisons, no officers to compel obedience or inflict punishment".* Though popular imagery might reduce this confederation to a union of small tribes, in the 16th century their population exceeded that of the Southern slave states—Virginia, Maryland, North Carolina, South Carolina, and Georgia.

Franklin's observations continue to yield a treasure trove of later-forgotten information: besides being hunters, builders, and warriors, the savages *"study oratory; the best speaker holds the most influence. Women cultivate the land, prepare food, nurture and raise children, and preserve the memory of public affairs. These occupations of men and women are considered natural and honorable. Having few artificial needs, they enjoy abundant leisure time to improve themselves through conversation. They consider our laborious way of life base and servile, and the knowledge we pride ourselves on frivolous and useless. An example of this occurred at the Treaty of Lancaster in Pennsylvania in 1744 between the Virginia Government and the Six Nations. After resolving the main matter, Virginia's commissioners informed the Indians that Williamsburg had a university with funds to educate Indian youth, and that if Six Nations chiefs sent half a dozen of their sons to this college, the government would ensure they were well provided for and instructed in all white people's knowledge. One of the Indians' rules of courtesy is never to respond to a public proposal on the same day it's made. They believe this would treat the matter as unimportant. To show respect, they take time to consider every proposal as something significant. Therefore, on that occasion too they deferred their response until the following day. When their spokesman began speaking, he expressed gratitude for the Virginia government's kindness in making this offer".*

The Iroquois spokesman's reply resonates today in a way any modern supremacist would find arrogant, while others of us find it profoundly wise, intelligent, and intellectually courageous:

*"We know"*, he said, *"you highly esteem the kind of learning taught in those colleges, and that the maintenance of our young men while with you would be very expensive. We are convinced you mean to do us good by your proposal, and we thank you heartily. But you who are wise must know that different nations have different conceptions of things, and we therefore hope you won't take offense if our ideas about education don't coincide with yours. We've had some experience in this matter. Several of our young people were educated in your colleges. They were instructed in your sciences, but when they returned to us they were ignorant of all means of living in nature. They couldn't endure cold or hunger, didn't know how to build a house, hunt deer, fight an enemy, or even speak our language properly. We appreciate your kind offer, but we cannot accept it. Now, to show our gratitude, if the gentlemen of Virginia will send us a dozen of their sons, we'll take great care with their education, instruct them in all we know, and make men of them."*

# LIBERAL DEMOCRACY: AN OXYMORON AND THREE HYPOTHESES

According to one of history's most robust interpretative theories—dialectical materialism—symbolic phenomena are expressions of a society's material base, its means of production and consumption. After Marx's death, his followers and critics introduced variations ranging from Max Weber to Marxists like Antonio Gramsci, Louis Althusser, and the Frankfurt School.

Twentieth-century Marxists refined the idea that the symbolic superstructure isn't merely a consequence of production and consumption conditions but possesses relative independence and influence over the material base. This Marxist critique of Marx generally established that these institutions, ideas, and ideologies—independent of economic systems—aimed, when dominant, to confirm the interests of the benefiting social class.

One concept I'd like to introduce here involves the strange and seemingly contradictory dialectic between (1) symbolic translations of societies' material base and (2) ideas that are, in principle, inconvenient or even foreign to it. I'm referring to the two dominant ideological dogmas of the Modern Era: *capitalism* and *democracy*. For generations, it's been common understanding in the United States that these are one and the same—just as socialism equals dictatorship, or capitalism equals Christianity.

Liberalism, the ideological articulation of former feudal lords and later slaveholders, opposed the concentrated political power of monarchies. It didn't oppose parliamentary monarchies protecting the new bourgeois elite (the old noble class), but rather absolutist monarchies (*dictatorships*) unresponsive to their direct control—

represented, as in imperial Athens, by a minority of the chosen, if not a hereditary senate. The purchase and hijacking of state power (monarchies) by their enemies, the liberal nobility, ensured the new ruling class a brutal repressive force against previous communal revolts and peasants dispossessed by land privatization through the *enclosure* system (*Flies in the Spiderweb*).

By definition, capitalism is anti-democratic, as its sole objective lies in capital concentration. No democracy is real if its citizens' freedom is limited to a minority giving orders and a majority receiving them. Without power there is no (social) freedom, and without money there is no power. Most members of capitalist society are wage-earners, professionals, or small merchants—meaning they are not capitalists. The power to decide, to legislate, to buy and sell goods, services, narratives, and wills is concentrated-privatized. In the United States and any neocolony, a handful of white men possess as much wealth as half the country and devote themselves to buying senators and presidents or directly writing laws. The model of slave societies remains intact: all have, as in the days of shackled slavery, constitutionally guaranteed freedom of expression (provided the formula $P=d.t$ is fulfilled); all have been equally united by the same mythological dogma (national and religious), by the same obedience to hard and effective work as the supreme value. Corporations that grew rich during slavery survived the legal abolition of the slave system by hijacking the libertarian sermon to present it as their own and claim credit for the freedoms that former shackled slaves enjoy today.

Historically, capitalism was always anti-democratic. Since its birth in the 17th century, in the name of market freedom, individual liberty, and democracy, capitalism specialized in destroying its subjects' and slaves' freedom. It took charge of destroying market freedom where it existed to impose the dictatorship of capital and empires. It took charge of destroying democracies, replacing them with banana dictators on every continent it vampirized by cannon force, through massacres and corruption of oppressed societies, only to then present itself as *the exemplary model* of development, freedom, and civilization.

Another problematic hypothesis here is: unlike Protestantism, *democracy contradicted the capitalist system from its material base.* Why would an idea, an ideology, become the banner of its opposite—capitalism and imperialism? How was it possible for democratic ideas to coexist so persistently with notions like racial superiority, as seen with Theodore Roosevelt and all imperialists of the Modern Era?

My first answer lies in how the Enlightenment reflected deep perplexity at discovering indigenous democracies in America and, as in previous cases, set out to hijack them. How? Through the Greek or "Western" antecedent. In fact, Rousseau, like Benjamin Franklin, knew the American democratic experiments perfectly well but chose to cite ancient Greeks instead. Franklin suffered the same racial prejudice. The assemblies of Ancient Greece (*Ecclesia*) consisted solely of male citizens, similar to American democracy during its first century. In both cases, only fifteen percent of inhabitants participated in elections. Within that percentage, another wealthier minority dominated.

Native American democracy, trafficked to Europe through Jesuit chronicles, must have had the same psychological and cultural impact as Vespucci's accounts in the new antagonistic tradition of social utopias, like Thomas More's *Utopia*. Depending on new ideas' power, the ruling class will either hijack or demonize them.

In Iroquois democracy, men and women had voice and vote in decisions reached by consensus. Every decision had to consider the "Seven Generations" principle. Athenian democracy was more individualistic, while indigenous systems established harmony between the One and the Whole, translating into greater political and social stability than in Greek or liberal democracies.

Perhaps the impact of the "American savages" experience was greater in 18th-century capitalist Europe because the continent's historical memory preserved a "vernacular" example—that of Greece—which over time became established as the natural replacement for absolute monarchies through the earlier tradition of feudal nobles, meaning modern liberals.

Another phenomenon we'll problematize as a working hypothesis can be summarized as follows: *All imperial systems are characterized by policies of cruelty* because their primary objective is the fear of losing control, even as they present themselves as civilized, like the Roman Pax or American Pax. We need only recall the spectacles of Roman cruelty in the circus, where the unequal fight between a gladiator (slave) and a lion excited both the emperor and the general public. Then we could continue with the cruelty of empires as diverse as the Mongol, the Aztec, or the more recent Anglo-Saxon empires with their invasions, wars, and massacres in colonies.

Is democracy (as in the millennia-old Iroquois case) incompatible with geopolitically dominant political systems? I believe it is.

# A Theory of Desocialization and Political Sadomasochism

According to various studies, children's self-esteem grew rapidly starting in the 1980s. In 1998 (Critique of Pure Passion) we wrote that parents had become obsessed with making their children believe they were Newton, Picasso, and Marilyn Monroe all in one, and that underlying this was fear of failure in a hyper-competitive civilization. Self-help publications had also multiplied, which only helped their authors sell many books.

Increasingly, the focus has been on the idea that happiness comes with individual success ("you can do it," "above all, love yourself"), and this success stems from competition. That is, both success and self-esteem concepts are based on the failure and humiliation of nearly everyone else, so it's no accident that people vote for narcissistic leaders who represent them.

How did we get here? For most of history, private property was limited to personal-use items like a house or a blacksmith's tools. The mere millennial existence of trade indicates a form of property recognized when exchanging Chinese silk for amber with an ant inside, the contraceptive plant silphium (origin of the heart symbol) for an aphrodisiac, a goat for ten Sumerian shekels, or a slave for a thousand denarii in the Roman Empire. But private property was very restricted and, in some cases, nonexistent. When it existed, it didn't apply to distant lands or abstract things as it did starting in the 17th century with the purchase of a hundredth share in a company exploiting resources on the other side of the world.

In the European Middle Ages, private property already existed extensively, but was a privilege restricted to the noble class. Peasants, artisans, servants, and occasional militiamen owned nothing: neither land nor surnames. Still, they had more rights than shackled slaves (and rights many wage-slaves today lack) to occupy the lord's land. They couldn't be evicted—not from altruism, but because serfs were more valuable than the land they worked.

Advertisement

The creation of money as a form of social interaction and the rise of the bourgeoisie democratized (access to) private property, both land and capital. It also disconnected serfs from land that was never theirs. The popularization of money liberated individuals from both land and social class. In this case, the possibility of upward mobility had a powerful impact on individual imagination—far more than in reality.

Soon, medieval nobles reorganized into liberals fighting against all centralization of power (monarchies, socialist states) that limited their own power to buy and sell things and human beings. That is, noble-liberals fought against the loss of social control caused by losing their monopoly on private property. In France they opposed monarchies. In England they allied with monarchy. Modern states that had theoretically emerged to protect common citizens from powerful abusers were immediately hijacked by these powerful actors who monopolized capital, finance, and investments—but couldn't monopolize police and military violence (as they had in the Middle Ages)—so they decided to buy it. As (almost) always, overproduction led to a concentration of power and violence by a minority that took various forms: minorities resulting from the intersection of particular conditions like ethnicity (the totem), sex, and social class.

One novelty introduced by capitalism was the *exchange value* independent from *use value*. This was a new step toward *abstraction* through the *dissociation-dislocation* of reality. The economy became separate from production, and then finance became separate from the economy, reaching the extreme of virtual currencies and "capital creation" out of thin air—that is, the extraction of others' value in a manner as symbolic as when a medieval archbishop built an opulent cathedral or a pharaoh claimed to be a god's son and convinced thousands of workers to move millions of multi-ton rocks to construct something as abstract as a pyramid to protect something as irrelevant as his own tomb.

Now, let us observe that if in the European Middle Ages private property was concentrated among a noble elite; if capitalism destroyed concentration based exclusively on class inheritance, it almost simultaneously began reproducing the previous order under new concepts and with new technologies. When private property became universalized, ironically, new minorities used this system to increase power concentration. In Mexico during the second half of the 19th century, the privatization of communal lands ended with 80 percent of peasants being dispossessed, since if land can be acquired with money, it can also be lost through money. The same happened in indigenous reservations in the United States during the same period. The same occurred when the shackled slavery system was abolished and freed slaves became wage slaves. Poor whites suffered the same fate. The British and Americans stated it explicitly: the new way to keep Black people in a system of slavery is to inoculate them with desires for things they don't need. (see *The Savage Frontier* or "Consumerism, Another Legacy of the Slave System")

Let's return to the psychological factor. The key lies not only in *desire* but also in *fear*. This uncertainty about tomorrow based on private property ownership created a new individual who desperately began accumulating, however meagerly, for their survival and their family's. Anxiety and fanaticism that produced both pain and pleasure. Accumulation at any cost became a sadomasochistic practice from which the individual could no longer escape.

If we observe other experiences, like that of Native Americans (socially more advanced than Europeans before their destruction), we can see that the center of the individual's social life was society itself. Even their dreams and desires could be political matters. The introduction of the dogma of private property and survival based on individual accumulation ("one's greed is everyone's prosperity") operated a *desocialization* of the individual. Their social relations came to depend on or be managed through the filter of self-interest in accumulation. Even the least greedy in any society were forced into this cannibalistic practice.

Individuals became desocialized, and in desocializing, they became dehumanized.

# THE WAR OF THE RICH AND UNIVERSAL WAGES

Neither democracy nor capitalism made the Northwest richer and more developed. Imperialism did. The difference between capitalism and democracy lies in their ethical, ideological, and social value principles. One is defined by its goal of power distribution (of freedom and societal benefits) and the other by its opposite: by its concentration in an increasingly smaller and more powerful minority.

Like all dominant systems, capitalism specialized not only in hijacking material goods but also symbolic ones—from politics, ideology, ethics, aesthetics, the narrative of its propaganda outlets and journalistic media to cultural means through the culture industry. Like all dominant systems, it reproduces as a fractal within each individual, each society, and the global order. On all three levels, there has always existed a parasitic relationship of a minority over a majority. Just as within a society the working class is parasitized (both physically and intellectually) by the ruling classes, this has always been the case between most countries and their parasitic empires.

To conceal or justify a position of dominance and exploitation, the slaveholder must demonize, demoralize, discredit, and "*denigrate*" the enslaved. This morality is also parasitic, since once inoculated into the oppressed organism, it feeds and reproduces within that very organism until producing fully realized slaves—unconditional defenders of their masters. Slaves who aspire to become masters, the oppressed who dream of becoming wealthy oppressors yet barely achieve being poor oppressors.

Among many dogmas, one that remains popular declares that "the poor are poor because they want to be," because "they don't try hard enough," "because they use drugs or drink alcohol," "because they don't work"—as if among the ruling, entrepreneurial, and political classes there were no drug addicts, alcoholics, lazy individuals, and idle rich, who nevertheless never fall from their privileged social status, much less end up living in poverty. Then, at any mobilization for social justice, the heirs of slaveholders and their second-rate imitators brandish their classist whip: *"go get a job, you bunch of bums."* The same accusations were leveled against indigenous workers in Bolivia's tin mines who died by age thirty, not only because they all suffered from pneumoconiosis ("black lung"), but because on their rare Sundays off, these uprooted men would go to village bars to get drunk and imagine love with a prostitute, scandalizing the local priest and upper-class ladies. The same for Black slaves in Brazil. The same for Mexicans in the United States, banana pickers in Central America, and the white gauchos in Argentina, according to Domingo Sarmiento. Poor slaves or rebellious freedmen were degenerates, layabouts, corrupt, and immoral.

This material-symbolic relationship hasn't changed since then. It has only transformed. The old myth collides head-on with reality yet always survives. Because the poor, the needy, those bound to miserable wages and the terror of losing them are easy prey for slavery—both physical and moral—and, as if that weren't enough, they're a market necessity: the more indoctrinated, the less educated, the less independent workers and consumers become, the more they increase capital's profits. This has been true from the days of banana republics to the virtual metaverse of investments and digital money. But like all laws, like all judicial rulings, like all money is symbolic without coercive force, this virtual world must be sustained by ancient military brutality—needless to say. A simple fact proves this: eradicating poverty in a country like the United States is cheap. With one percent of national GDP (25% of the Pentagon's annual budget; less than 3% of what was spent on the war in Afghanistan), poverty could be completely eradicated.

Eradicating poverty worldwide would cost between $70 and $325 billion annually—less than 0.5% of OECD countries' GDP. Still, experts agree that to combat poverty more efficiently, better than a plan for the poor is a universal plan.

Exactly the same logic applies not only to keeping wages and small business opportunities perpetually depressed, but to preventing or postponing the great threat looming over parasitic elites—to name just one factor that will accelerate the 21st century revolution: universal basic income. The Great Revolution of this century is being delayed by fascist reaction—capitalism's and dying empires' last resort, violent, genocidal, and moribund.

A World Bank study showed that the overwhelming majority of poor people who received free income didn't spend it on alcohol or tobacco. On the contrary, after some time, consumption of these stimulants decreased. Of course, such data isn't welcome to those who feel their privileges threatened or aren't sufficiently revered for the taxes they pay. Another study from Ohio University published in 2009 collected the most common criticism against redistribution programs: "*In Nicaragua, other negative opinions and misunderstandings about the RPS circulated. A high-ranking official from the Ministry of Family reported that the RPS only gave cash payments, and that husbands would wait for their wives to return to take the money and spend it on alcohol*". In May 2014, the World Bank itself echoed this idea and ultimately refuted it in a study that included dozens of field studies. The report answered its central question right in the title:

"*Do the Poor Waste Money on Alcohol and Cigarettes? No.*" In fact, although not significantly, consumption of these stimulants decreased. The World Bank study concluded: "*We should stop worrying about how the poor misuse their transfer income. They don't spend it on alcohol and cigarettes but on chocolates.*"

Various studies and state-run experiments have demonstrated a truth so simple it's not considered as such but rather dismissed as mere tautology: "*the main reason the poor are poor is because they have no money.*" Every time one mentions this "discovery" articulated by several contemporary sociologists and historians, they must pause for a few seconds until the laughter gives way to more reflective silence. A *The Lancet* study in Namibia concluded that when the poor receive unconditional income, they tend to work harder than when told what they must do to deserve it.

As we previously analyzed in *Flies in the Web*, the Universal Basic Income proposal has a contradictory and paradoxical precedent. During World War II, Juliet Rhys-Williams, a member of the Liberal Party (then England's left-wing), proposed a "negative income tax" whereby anyone earning below a minimum subsistence line would receive a subsidy inversely proportional to their income. That is, if we consider an ascending income curve and intersect it with a horizontal line defining a subsistence minimum, all those below the line should receive enough to reach that minimum, while others should pay progressively more as their income rises. Naturally, progressive taxation is a long-established practice, but not the first part. In his book *Where Do We Go from Here: Chaos or Community?* (1967), Martin Luther King foresaw the solution: "*We must create full employment or create incomes. I'm convinced the simplest approach will prove most effective: the solution to poverty is to abolish it directly through a measure now widely discussed—the guaranteed income.*"

In 1964, while Lyndon Johnson escalated his imperialist war against Vietnam and the CIA did likewise in Africa and Latin America—as Democrats (the imperialist left) typically do—they showed more humanity domestically. The "War on Poverty" program included social experiments very similar to universal basic income, something even neoliberalism's guru, economist Milton Friedman, didn't oppose. Quite the contrary, when he proposed his "negative income tax."[1]

The results were positive, though interpreted negatively. There was a nine percent decrease in wage labor, but among young mothers and poor youth, high school graduation rates rose by thirty percent. Researchers found even that nine percent figure was inflated—likely due to people's fear of losing benefits, various home-based work arrangements, and most probably because many young people had chosen to continue studying, as reflected in the earlier graduation percentage.

The idea of eliminating poverty through federally funded programs gained more popular and media support than putting a man on the Moon. Of course, not everyone agreed, and in 1978 the miracle many awaited occurred. One case study in Seattle recorded a fifty percent increase in divorces. Economic freedom often produces such outcomes. Women were growing accustomed to too much freedom. This possibility alone derailed the experiment, which wasn't corrected when it was later discovered the fifty percent figure resulted from a statistical miscalculation.

Perhaps the most systematic social experiment on universal basic income was conducted in 1973 in the small Canadian town of

---

[1] See *Flies in the Spiderweb. A History of the Commercialization of Existence—and Its Means* (Majfud, Humanus, 2023), p. 606.

Dauphin. A few years earlier, Dutch historian Rutger Bregman (currently a defender of "kind capitalism") popularized it in his book *Utopia for Realists*. From 1974 to 1978, a thousand families in Dauphin received an unconditional salary equivalent to $20,000 annually in today's dollars. In the general elections four years later, conservatives won and the project was abandoned. There wasn't even budget allocated to analyze the collected data. Politicians concluded on their own that the experiment had failed. Researchers packed all the gathered data into two thousand boxes, and the project was forgotten. Thirty years later, it was discovered in an attic and rescued from imminent destruction. The researcher who uncovered this treasure, economist Evelyn Forget, compared the project's data with other realities and concluded the experiment had been a resounding success, contradicting all opposing arguments: families didn't devote themselves to having more children (decades ago the fear wasn't childless whites as in the 19th century but poor people with children) and children's school performance improved. Domestic violence declined and hospitalizations for other reasons decreased by 8.5 percent.

Universal income experiments didn't end there. They multiplied with identical results. In 2009, the city of London concluded it had spent over half a million pounds on thirteen homeless people through police and social workers. When each was offered £3,000 unconditionally, the result wasn't just reduced city spending to £50,000 on the same individuals—more than half voluntarily escaped that cycle of misery. They invested in their own needs like hygiene, housing, and in some cases, gardening classes. Similar experiments occurred in Namibia, Rwanda, Kenya and Uganda, where men and women in extreme poverty received cash, mostly unconditionally, with positive outcomes: many invested in small businesses like purchasing motorcycles for taxi services, which in turn improved communication and transportation for other villagers, multiplying income not just for direct recipients but their neighbors too.

As University of Manchester researchers demonstrate, in other cases simply reducing child malnutrition led to increased physical height and IQ; improved school performance; and reduced poverty and crime by tens of percentage points. Naturally, it also reduced child labor and modern slavery that always benefited the wealthiest in those societies and globally, like the current mass slavery in Congo's cobalt mines. Similar experiences were replicated across dozens of countries from Latin America to Asia, facing identical resistance and discrediting from upper classes and declining imperial nations. [2]

What's the secret? The answer echoes my own 1996 experience in Mozambique. The poor weren't given life plans by national or foreign (white) aid workers—who often perform missionary-like work teaching them how to stop being poor—but received economic resources (money) they could manage according to their own perceived needs. Nobody (unless crossing into delusion or social dysfunction after years of dehumanization) knows more about their immediate and long-term needs than those experiencing them. In other words, poverty's cause isn't cultural—it's economic and,

---

[2] This extensive study was directed by Joseph Hanlon and published under the title *Just Give Money to the Poor: The Development Revolution from the Global South*. United Kingdom, Kumarian Press, 2010. I met Hanlon and traveled through Mozambique with him in 1996. I spent evenings conversing in Portuguese with him and his wife Therese in houses without electricity on various islands, in old Portuguese homes surrounded by marijuana fields.

fundamentally, political. This material reality later transforms into a culture that lower-class detractors mistake as poverty's cause.

We've insisted for years on the same principle for any nation's development: first it must cease being a colony, then become independent—greater independence means greater development. This is proven throughout global history, even just considering Latin American countries' developmental differences since the 19th century: the wealthier they were, the more desired by empires, and consequently, the less developed.

The same logic applies to something we've analyzed in prior studies (and here too we haven't reinvented the wheel): capitalism emerged from the European discovery of America by Spaniards and Portuguese. It was born through massive capital plunder (gold, silver, copper, iron, guano, meat, wheat and all necessary raw materials) that made possible new European social classes—first merchants in the Netherlands, then proletarians in England. It was this same plunder—ironically carried out and imposed by the ideologues of the "free market"—that made possible another birth: the English Industrial Revolution, a century after destroying the most prosperous nations of its time (India, Bangladesh, later China and much of the Middle East) through cannon fire, drugs, and collaborationism. The European Industrial Revolution emerged generations after aborting the birth of industrial revolutions in Asia.

The discovery of America and the plundering of overseas resources was the trigger and necessary sustenance for European development, which continued through the destruction, looting, and parasitism of other continents—a parasitism that persists today, albeit on a smaller scale by the declining yet still violent Western empires.

The same can be said of freedom of expression: give global citizens economic security and watch how many truths come to light, displacing the myths perpetuated by dominant classes and nations. Naturally, these truths aren't automatic products of any system, as we'll always need truly free spirits (free to think, free from greed), but undoubtedly the difference from our current suffering would be astronomical.

Much of the criticism and fears surrounding Universal Basic Income stem from anxiety that masses of people will stop working. This fear stems from capitalism's inherent corruption: nobody moves unless money is involved. Universal Basic Income is such a modest proposal that it doesn't even advocate abolishing money or capitalism's passion for accumulating wealth. That would belong to a higher stage of human development—if we're capable of achieving something better than this. Unlike welfare programs that beneficiaries lose upon improving their circumstances, universal income has the virtue of stimulating work and creativity.

# Education for More Efficient Slavery

My grandfather was a farmer who didn't read books, but (like most of his generation) valued education as the primary instrument of liberation. The subsequent generation felt the same. My parents, besides being merchants and laborers, were high school and vocational school teachers. Among their trophies was having taught students who became Uruguayan cultural icons like Eduardo Darnauchans and Eduardo Larbanois.

My father and his father-in-law maintained an intense dialogue, mostly by telephone since they lived at opposite ends of Uruguay, continuing for two decades after my mother's death until my grandfather passed. Despite ideological differences (my grandfather a socialist, my father a capitalist), they shared certain fundamental values. This tolerance was more pronounced in Uruguay than elsewhere in the hemisphere, largely stemming from Enlightenment culture promoted since the 19th century through free education by J.P. Varela and J. Batlle y Ordóñez.

Both consumed newspaper journalism but almost never read books. Yet their respect for enlightened education was absolute. My father, a carpenter, would trade debts for books.

"Why books," I'd ask, "if you never read them?"

"Doesn't matter," he'd say. "Books harm no one, and sooner or later, they'll serve someone."

His small library featured Shakespeare, encyclopedias, and technical manuals—some Soviet translations. When soldiers smashed through my bedroom ceiling searching for my grandfather's "subversive materials," it never occurred to them to open a library book.

The continent's fascist dictatorships imposed the idea that books could be dangerous. They didn't just burn them—they disappeared their readers. This idea had actually been inoculated by the CIA (most famously through Operation Mockingbird), applying Marxist Antonio Gramsci's theories while blaming Gramscians for "brainwashing" educated people. Gramsci had diagnosed reality, just as Marx's *class struggle* was less a prescription than a historical and social diagnosis. One would have to be blind not to see it today.

Nazi Göring is credited with the phrase: "When I hear the word culture, I reach for my revolver." In the early 1960s, Nobel laureate Cesar Milstein recalled a military government minister declaring Argentina wouldn't improve until two million intellectuals were expelled. When Milstein and his intellectual cohort were expelled in the sixties, Argentina had been on par with Australia and Canada. Fascism, always so clumsy with ideas, attributed Latin America's underdevelopment to the poor reading *Open Veins of Latin America* by Galeano. Galeano dedicated his life to criticizing the powerful; the powerful never defended themselves, because others dedicated their lives to criticizing Galeano.

Contemporary neofascism is simply an expression of the neofeudal order of the global economy and the frustrations of declining empires, just as it was a century ago. But their strategies have been updated: they no longer burn books or kidnap writers as during Nazi Germany or Pinochet's Chile. Now they're presented as useless or irrelevant—when not outright banned by law, as in the United States.

The *influencers* have multiplied the illusion of atomized freedom among *entrepreneurs* who, for a hundred or a thousand dollars (with no retirement contributions, no rights to vacations, healthcare or education) humiliate a beggar for a few hundred *likes*.

Another whip lashes against universities and public schools, which the Bush family began privatizing in the 80s with their *charter* school model. As always, the genius was in siphoning money from the hated State to defund public education and present private alternatives as the solution.

Since then, the hatred and contempt for universities—paradoxically emerging against the world's most prestigious university system—added a new strategy. Writers like Andrés Oppenheimer summarized it in the cliché: "We need more engineers and fewer philosophers." Why not "We need more engineers and fewer successful businessmen, lobbyists and financial cults"?

My first university degree was in architecture. Thanks to Uruguay's education system, I could spend years calculating reinforced concrete structures and some time as a high school math teacher. We can agree that the U.S., Europe or Latin America need more engineers, but since when are engineering and philosophy incompatible? Why can't an engineer be a philosopher and vice versa?

The heart of the problem is called *education*, not *training* hijacked by the ideological interests of the world's owners. The attack on humanities, philosophy and arts doesn't come from scientists or engineers with broad culture; it comes from "successful businessmen" who are always men and always successful because they manage to hijack the States they hate.

This utilitarian ideology has, as its undeclared objective, confirming and controlling wage slaves. Exactly what 19th century slavers preached and practiced in freedom's name: slaves should *specialize* in one productive, useful activity pleasing to God, for their own good and for *their* country's. Whenever a slave learned to read, they were punished. If they wrote memoirs, like Juan Manzano, they were tortured. If the slave *prospered*, they were applauded. If they spent free time on some *useless*, liberating, humanist education, they were demonized. Hence many slaves staunchly defended slavery and persecuted free men daring to question the system's definitions of *freedom*. The masters didn't even bother moralizing—they always had professional sycophants to do it better.

We've returned to that moment. In Uruguay, the attack on enlightened, liberating education has its promoters. Also its defenders, like my friend Pablo Romero García, one of the most knowledgeable education experts—tainted by the sin of being a philosophy professor. *Encomenderos* like President Milei in Argentina and his horde of anti-Enlightenment barbarians attacked public universities (independent of noble capital) from day one.[3] Having no ideas, they copy what's already growing stale in the U.S. while creating demons to pose as saintly saviors—just like the Middle Ages.

Meanwhile in the U.S., libertarian capitalists keep blaming socialism (born in universities) for all their ills while promoting anti-Enlightenment and *enslaving utilitarianism* as the final solution. The solution of barbarism and slavery—always in the name of *freedom*, of course.

---

[3] *Encomenderos*: (from "encomienda"). Spanish colonists who were granted the right to exploit labor from Indigenous people in the Spanish.

# THE TROTSKY OF THE BRONX

In 1916, the Russian ship Askold docked in the port of Marseille. Shortly after, a mutiny onboard resulted in the murder of an officer, forcing French authorities to intervene. During inspection, they found several copies of the Russian newspaper *Nashe Slovo* (*Our Word*), published by Trotsky and considered anti-Russian literature by the regime of Nicholas II. Questioned by French authorities, Trotsky argued the copies had been planted by Russian officers.

In October, without explanation, French authorities entered his apartment at 31 Rue de la Pompe in Paris and took him away, leaving his wife Natalya and their two children to fend for themselves. The detainee was suspected of opposing the war. They took him to the Spanish border and left him on the other side, in the Basque Country. In San Sebastián he was arrested again without legal justification and taken to Madrid, where days later—after a visit to the Prado Museum—he was imprisoned and then transferred to Cádiz with the intention of deporting him to Cuba.

Trotsky had no doubts: Spanish authorities were following orders from French authorities, who were following orders from Russian authorities, who were following orders from French banks that had invested too heavily in Nicholas II's dictatorship. In jail, he began studying English while awaiting negotiations by his friends (among Spanish republicans and American socialists) who saw no other solution to his exile trajectory than the New World. Finally, the efforts succeeded, and authorities approved his journey to the United States.

During the mandatory interrogation before boarding, he stated he was not an anarchist, polygamist, alcoholic, or mentally impaired, and had never lived in a charity home—necessary conditions, aside from being white, for immigration authorities at the time. He even lied by claiming he had never been imprisoned. Trotsky had been jailed many times under Tsarist Russia—for writing, for organizing workers' unions, and for organizing protests against the 1905 massacre of a thousand demonstrators in St. Petersburg.

Natalya also lied to the immigration officer: she had been imprisoned for attending a workers' gathering in St. Petersburg commemorating May Day and the Chicago workers' massacre. By then, the brutal dictatorship of Tsar Nicholas II (Emperor of Russia, King of Poland, and Grand Duke of Finland) had not only persecuted all manner of dissidents but had left nearly half a million dead in the 1891-92 famine. Nicholas II, a recognized nationalist and antisemite like his predecessors, would have been Hitler's primary ally had he not been overthrown by the October Revolution—or November, depending on the calendar used. This historical factor likely contradicted Karl Marx's prediction: it would not be an industrialized society where the proletariat seized power, but an agrarian and medieval one like Russia's. Nicholas II's father had executed Lenin's older brother by hanging, and the October Revolution, led by Lenin, executed Nicholas II. A century later, the tsar and his family would be canonized as martyr saints by the Russian Orthodox Church.

Trotsky had adopted that name from his jailer in Siberia in 1902, but in 1917 he managed to travel to New York under his original surname, Bronstein. After a 17-day voyage, the steamship announced arrival in New York at 3:00 AM. It stopped at Ellis Island, the mandatory checkpoint where, under the gaze of the Statue of

Liberty, immigrants had to prove they were healthy, did not enjoy alcohol, and—if possible—were white. Those traveling first class didn't even need to disembark, as officers came to their cabins. Such was the case for the Trotsky family. Beyond Immigration, they were warmly received by several publishers and Socialist Party members. The party's lawyer and Marxist theorist, Louis Boudin, took them to dinner.

Meanwhile, Lenin continued his exile through newspapers from his own refuge in Switzerland. Trotsky had broken with Lenin in 1902 over ideological and personal differences. To Trotsky, Lenin was a "terrible egotist." To Lenin, Trotsky was a "Judas," an "evasive trickster." For Lenin, there could be no proletarian revolution without a revolutionary vanguard and a centralized state to lead a profound societal reform before ascending to higher levels of social justice. Trotsky, less pragmatic, leaned closer to the anarchists, rejecting vertical structures in favor of grassroots popular organizations like unions and popular assemblies—the *soviets*. For Trotsky, Lenin's idea of a "dictatorship *of* the proletariat and *of* the peasants" was more accurately a "dictatorship *over* the proletariat and peasants."

The principle that united them was simple: wars are products of national bourgeoisies (just as in the Middle Ages they were products of nobility, not peasants—the pawns on the chessboard) and are fueled by nationalisms, much like religion once served as a unifying element. At the time, many socialists and anarchists believed that the unity of the world's workers would eliminate the root cause of the greatest injustices and tragedies in a world where laborers and their children marched to kill other workers in the name of a nation and for the benefit of ruling classes. World War I only confirmed this thesis: workers from some countries united against workers from neighboring nations, driven by nationalist fanaticism that brought them no benefit—only death, destruction, and poverty.

In 1917, New York remained a kind of anarchist republic. Newspapers and books were published in dozens of languages, from Spanish to Russian. Theater plays were performed by actors from various countries for diverse communities. *Novy Mir* (*New World*), a weekly published in Russian from a modest workshop at 77 Saint Marks Place in Staten Island, was simultaneously Bolshevik and Menshevik. Lenin often read *Novy Mir* during his Swiss exile, so he learned of Trotsky's reception in America. *"Had I been the King of England, they couldn't have treated me better,"* Trotsky remarked.

Various newspapers announced his arrival in New York aboard the Monserrat. The Trotsky family had been expelled from Russia, Austria, Germany, France, and finally Spain at the request of the Russian diplomatic network—a fact newspapers seized as a headline. "Expelled from Four Countries," declared the *New York Times* on January 15th, on its second page. For his anti-war and anti-nationalist preaching, the nation's leading paper labeled him a socialist, Marxist, and *"Russian pacifist"* arriving with his wife and two sons—Leon, 11, and Serge, 9. On the same page, the New York Times reported a purge of progressives from the Tsar's Russian government, replaced by far-right supporters. The socialist Yiddish daily *The Jewish Daily Forward*, with a circulation exceeding 200,000 copies daily, featured Trotsky on its January 16th front page.

Trotsky stayed two months in a Bronx apartment on Wise Avenue. On November 4th, after his return to Russia, Baltimore's *The Sun* described Trotsky as an anarcho-socialist and the second most important figure in the Russian Revolution after Lenin. Months later, in September, the *Bronx Home News* would headline: "A Bronx Man Leads the Russian Revolution."

In New York, salons served as refuges for socialists and anarchists expelled from Europe—often later tried and convicted in America too. For some reason, the racist right wing—whether the Ku Klux Klan, the powerful industrialists of the era (soon replaced by *Nazis* and *fascists*; decades later, *neoliberals*; a century on, *libertarians*)—were rare birds in these gatherings of cultured folk. Race, homeland, and money have always been the right's bastions. Culture and non-commercial thought never were. Hence their traditional obsession with demonizing or eliminating arts, humanities, sciences, and non-profit universities.

Theodore Roosevelt believed anarchists (foreigners) were seizing control of the country—or wanted voters to believe this theory as a classic electoral strategy—so he ordered close surveillance of anyone suspected of anarchist ties. In 1908, the Bureau of Investigation was created under the guise of being an ideological police force rather than a federal crime investigation agency. In 1924, J. Edgar Hoover became director of the Bureau of Investigation, which nine years later would become the FBI. Hoover would not relinquish his position—nor his obsession with persecuting all manner of individuals with ideas or sentiments outside the national dogma (socialists and lesbians alike)—until his death in 1972, nearly half a century later.

In New York, Trotsky discovered his popularity across the Atlantic. The socialist newspaper published in German since 1878, *New Yorker Volkszeitung*, recorded Trotsky's remarks such as: "*I am stateless, and I am glad to have found a country that has accepted me within its borders.*" In fact, he was surprised to find an open political and intellectual atmosphere, free from censorship and persecution. In other words, the polar opposite of what the United States would become decades later—colonized by religious fanaticism and Protestant obsessions over faith, which would manifest as

McCarthyism in the 1950s and all manner of ideological persecution by the media, J. Edgar Hoover's FBI, Allen W. Dulles's CIA, and others, perfect representatives of America's ideological police.

The Russian Revolution did not handle press freedom much differently. The same Trotsky who had acknowledged this kind of freedom in New York became, months later, the second most important leader of the new USSR after Lenin. As Foreign Minister of a government that banned not only conservative newspapers but even socialist ones, he participated in this suppression.

There will always be excuses to limit freedom of expression, but history shows it is a luxury of dominant regimes—those against which criticism has no chance of effecting real change, as was the case with the British and American empires. This is evidenced by their constitutional protections even during slavery and anti-imperialist critiques within these empires, like John Hobson in England and Mark Twain in America, to name just two (see $P=d.t$).

# Imperial Democracies, Solidary Dictatorships

History leaves little room for exceptions: under the banner of *democracy*, nations were plundered; under the cry of *freedom*, slavery expanded alongside the most brutal and industrialized forms of imperialism. Nearly always, this was perpetuated by democracies, not dictatorships. It is no accident that Theodore Roosevelt wrote that *"the democracy of this century needs no further justification for its existence than the simple fact that it has been organized so the white race may take possession of the finest lands of the New World."*

Generally, colonial and postcolonial dictatorships (almost all functional dictatorships, and resistant ones only by exception) were the logical consequence of these democratic empires. All following an ancient logic. In classical Greece, Athens was a democracy strikingly similar to those of recent centuries: it maintained temporary slaves, tolerated some diversity, and boasted of accepting immigrants from other peoples; a select few voted, and its domination over other Greek city-states like Sparta rested on the power of its wealth. Two thousand years later, modern empires always afforded themselves the luxury of flaunting democracy, tolerance for diversity, and acceptance of dissent within their borders... Naturally, so long as their power faced no competition and they continued imposing the opposite in their colonies (where criticism was more dangerous) for the economic benefit of the civilized metropole.

The modern history of so-called democracies—as systems-of-power-sharing-among-the-dominant-class, unified by their capitals and oligopolies—reveals they were more dictatorial, imperialistic, and brutal toward other nations than actual dictatorships. Perhaps

because they were driven by the arrogance of considering themselves benevolent. Perhaps because nearly all these empires were
capitalist. This was the case (for both reasons) with the brutal British, Dutch, French, and American empires. It continues today with
the warmongering of NATO—composed of liberal democracies all
hijacked by financial elites, just as they once were by industrial capital. Further on the periphery, for instance, one of the most recur-
rent arguments justifying Israel's prolonged and brutal apartheid is
that the country "is the only democracy in the Middle East." Even if
this were a full democracy and not a limited one, it neither author-
izes nor justifies its government in dispossessing another nation—
Palestine—at its whim through military force, effectively denying
political existence to an entire people under the pretext that some in
their independence resistance do not recognize Israel's existence.

Why have the world's greatest dictatorships been national democracies, while dictatorships like Cuba's or Libya's, on the contrary, stood in solidarity with colonies and the oppressed peoples of
the world? What explains this (apparent) paradox? Could it be that
dictators were more cautious, fearing loss of power? Perhaps because
those dictatorships emerged from struggles against the genocidal
brutality of imperialisms? Or maybe what we call *democracy* isn't the
democracy of Native Americans (like the Iroquois Confederacy before civilized settlers destroyed it), but something entirely different:
democracy as Anglo-Saxons understood and fossilized it—based on
dispossession, the displacement of others, and the defense of private
property?

This occurred with ancient Athenian democracy and with
Northwestern democracies of the Modern Era. The victims are always guilty of threatening their masters, who receive compensation
for any economic losses whenever slavery is abolished or a colony

gains independence. Thus, the invaded become the invaders. The massacred are deemed violent. The corrupted are called corrupt. Those assaulted, starved, and exterminated for centuries to benefit developed nations remain solely responsible for their own poverty.

# Culture for Liberation

Art and culture have played a crucial role in human existence and survival for at least 75,000 years. They're what made us human. Often, culture has faced destruction by barbarism—from ancient library burnings to fascist book burnings in modern times, or today's book bans and censorship of even Michelangelo's nude David in the United States.

Yet when discussing culture, we often mistakenly assume it's neutral or positive. Followers of the Confederacy that fought to preserve slavery claim they're defending their cultural rights, omitting that this was a culture of enslavement. Many Spaniards defend bull torture as traditional art and culture. Pleasure or indifference toward others' suffering constitutes fascist culture—the exact opposite of what we understand as art and culture.

We understand art as a radical expression of freedom. No creation exists without freedom. As expression (pressure from within), artists interpret, challenge, anticipate, or shape collective fears and dreams—just as dreams shape our deepest needs. Commercial art, anti-art, anesthetizes. Its function is distraction (to divert, detach, distance)—the brothel before returning to wage slavery's dehumanizing path. Unconditional, unqualified art awakens, unsettles, moves, refuses oblivion. Art makes us freer. Art completes us, humanizes us. As culture's exploratory vanguard, art doesn't merely reflect—above all, it creates. It creates meaning, creates realities, creates history.

Yet even if we explain what art means to us, the task remains incomplete, for art ultimately defines itself through that "something more" existing only in concrete works. A glance at millennia of pre-served artworks reveals art isn't market, politics, religion, or moral-ity—yet remains deeply engaged with all these human dimensions. Without them, it's very little or nothing at all.

While unqualified art is too rebellious for superior orders, strict formulas, or any commitments, artists—as sensitive members of so-ciety—aren't indifferent to engagement: commitment to human-ity's daily renewal, to fighting barbarism's pain and indifference; commitment to reclaiming pleasure and happiness, to attempting flight beyond freedom's economic, social, ideological, or existential constraints.

Art and culture—as humanity's deepest form of knowledge and dialogue across peoples and generations—aren't luxuries but neces-sities. Especially in a world that, for the first time in history, has placed human existence in question. Beyond reductive consumer-ism, culture proves crucial for rescuing dehumanized, one-dimen-sional societies and individuals—stuffed like sausages with commercial junk. It is also essential for the survival of the biosphere itself, of which humans are only a part. A small part, yet lethal.

For non-commercial culture, as with the great spiritual move-ments throughout history across all continents, solidarity, altruism, and open dialogue with others have been central, foundational. Only in recent generations—marked and wounded by the ideology of the most savage individualistic success-worship—could an idea like selfishness become "a superior moral value," while altruism ended up being defined as humanity's enemy according to Ayn Rand, an idea now echoed by messiahs and messengers of capital as the sole moral currency. This historical degeneration confused the individual with individualism, forgetting that no individual exists without society. It is society that gives individuals their entire meaning, even for those sickened by the pathology of wealth, accumulation, and the fiction of individual success.

Art has survived thanks to artists who barely survive outside commercial circuits, powerful media monopolies, and promotional machinery. This task has been and remains historic. It is the last frontier of resistance against barbarism, which simplifies everything to sell it faster—all in the name of "freedom of choice," as promised by McDonald's menu.

But this task becomes impossible when artists cease to survive or abandon their deepest vocation to feed their children, or simply succumb to the demoralization of dominant barbarism—which isn't any specific government but the global tyranny of capital concentrated in some dark corner of the world. Virtual capitals that materialize from nothing, as fictitious as a Borges tale, yet without the honesty to admit it.

This is why societies must, first, become aware to protect themselves against discourses justifying their own enslavement, and second, take action. The most urgent and effective action has always been unity. It's no accident that hegemonic ideology attacks all forms of organized unity while promoting individualism under promises of salvation, as destruction accumulates by the roadside unnoticed by alienated individuals.

To see, to hear the effects of barbarism—this has always been the role of art and culture. Power knows this. That's why it has always tried to buy them, corrupt them with money, or outright eliminate them through discredit, mockery, demonization, and the economic ruin of true artists.

Rarely has the agony of art and culture so coincided with this particular moment for our species—threatened with extinction for the first time in recorded history and prehistory, not by an external threat but by our own hegemonic system that deifies individual profits over all collective demands.

Threatened by the culture of death. Death-in-life and its culture must be fought with the culture of freedom, with artists' commitment to Humanity, starting with the rescue of that poor word, *freedom*, kidnapped and abused by the culture of death sold as the only path to happiness—the happiness of consumption, of drug-like pleasure or indifference to others' suffering.

# THE UNSHAKABLE FAITH OF SUBJECTS

The richest man in human history (according to *Time* magazine and scholars) visited the Middle East only once. It was in 1324, when the Islamic Empire still represented what centuries later Westerners would call the First World in reference to themselves. Various witnesses, including Syrian historians, detailed the impression left by Mali's powerful king during his year-long pilgrimage.

Mansa Musa crossed Africa along its widest parallel, carrying so much gold in his treasury that upon reaching Egypt, his generosity to the poor he encountered along the way caused inflation lasting ten years.

Four centuries later, Irish banker Richard Cantillon discovered that money issuance always benefited the wealthy closest to power, as they could buy and invest before inflationary waves reached them. Unlike modern inflations—where money creation occurs at the pyramid's peak and its creators call it "the poor man's tax"—the inflation Musa triggered couldn't have been so bad for the poor, since they were the first to receive gold, benefiting before inflation trickled upward. A true oddity in economic history, about which I'm unaware of any academic discussions.

In the late 19th century, William Jennings Bryan, the Democratic candidate supported by the left-wing *Populist Party* and U.S. labor unions, proposed issuing and distributing silver dollars to overcome the deep recession. The proposal was criminalized by banks and large corporations because the measure would create inflation. For indebted farmers and workers, the word *inflation* didn't frighten them. Quite the opposite. Higher inflation would benefit them. Not to mention a redistribution of wealth accumulated by few families during the so-called Gilded Age that preceded the Progressive Era.

The banks hired writer Theodore Roosevelt, later known as the gentle president with the big stick, to paint Bryan as a radical who wanted to turn workers against the rich. Intimidated by massive rhetoric, business owners posted signs at factory entrances warning that *if young Bryan were elected president, their factories would close*. Bryan lost the election—the first where massive corporate propaganda showed its teeth.

Mansa Musa and his tourist-rich fortune traveled protected by an army of guards and ten thousand slaves. Debates still survive today about the number of slaves, though none about who they were. Civilized Western literature calls *slaves* those serving others, and *employees* their own slaves. Those slaves, like today's wage slaves, weren't enslaved due to their race nor was their slavery hereditary— two perversions that the West added not many centuries ago to justify buying and selling human beings like donkeys or financial stocks. In any case, each of Musa's slaves or servants carried a small fortune of nearly two kilos of gold.

This distant fact always impressed me, though it wasn't unusual. Without any effort, the guards and their servants could have taken Musa prisoner. They could have killed him or abandoned him in the Sahara sands, where he would have perished from unknown hardships. In Mali, *in absentia*, an even greater conspiracy could have replaced him in power, and his incalculable fortune in pure gold could have easily been redistributed among new elites or the people themselves.

While none of this would have been unthinkable historically, judging by events it apparently was for his subjects. What prevented them from yielding to individual temptation or collective justice?

Mansa Musa was protected by his subjects' belief—a protection no modern weapon could have provided during his journey from Mali to Egypt and then Mecca. This belief in the myth of power is likely responsible for the *status quo* of every social and economic system throughout history, including capitalism.

For centuries—from Father Bartolomé de las Casas to Simón Bolívar to American abolitionists—slaves participated in resisting their own liberation. What prevented them from rebelling against their minority masters? Partly the whip and firearms in white hands, as proven in some rare rebellions, but these failed because they weren't massive. They weren't massive because the white masters' preaching and moralizing were more effective than their whips. When rebellions succeeded, as in 1804 Haiti, they were crushed by the silent presence of French and American imperial cannons.

The end of chattel slavery didn't begin through slave rebellion, but through activism by a few free citizens and the inconvenience of the old slave system for new industrial masters in the North who preferred wage slaves as a cheaper, more convenient alternative for production and consumption. Fear of the master, blind faith in a leader or system, only breaks through an imbalance that rhetoric can't repair.

A second observation emerges from Musa's story. Despite his massive wealth accumulation, history—both of his time and contemporary—remembers him as a generous leader. This doesn't mean Musa was especially kind-hearted, any more than Bill Gates is through his philanthropic hobby. It means humanity has always valued generosity and altruism as crucial values for species survival and collective happiness. Generosity, altruism, compassion, and empathy for the needy have always been supreme values since the dawn of civilization and likely since the Paleolithic era. Otherwise, we wouldn't be here today—me writing these words and you reading them.

Since biblical and pre-war times, the accumulation of wealth by a few in a community with poor people was considered a sin. Prophets like Amos and Jesus were demonized for denouncing this form of social injustice. Wise rulers were those who canceled the unpayable debts of the lower classes, with that torch-bearing gesture that later became the Statue of Liberty in Manhattan, atop verses proclaiming "give me your tired, your poor"—another monument to modern emptiness.

In other words, our era is marked by a historical anomaly: the valuation of selfishness and cruelty as virtues, while solidarity and altruism are dismissed—as Milei declared in Washington ("social justice is violent") and writers like Ryan Ann formulated in 1964: *"evil is compassion, not selfishness"*.

All these qualities our time has demonized as individual weaknesses, societal immoralities, while elevating psychopaths like Elon Musk and drug-addled Nazis with fortunes rivaling Argentina's GDP—greater than Malaysia's or Colombia's—to heroic status.

# THE MOST PERVERSE DOGMA OF MODERN HISTORY

It's striking how ideological dogmas later passed off as "common sense" or "pragmatism"—these fictional decorations—always miss the broader historical framework, fixating instead on a single puzzle piece.

In the video I include here, Margaret Thatcher cites examples like Russia and Congo, underdeveloped despite their natural resources, "because they lacked an entrepreneurial economy." Of course they had one—in Africa, Latin America, and other Global South regions, entrepreneurial freedom (I mean real capitalist entrepreneurs, not small business owners living off their labor) and capital mobility faced fewer restrictions than in European or U.S. governments. These were capitalist economies directly serving brutal extractive empires like hers—Britain (which explains their current decline, now blamed on immigrants; blindly, as in this case of blind pride for one's own development and prosperity).

True to neoliberal dogma, whether from masters or collaborators, Mrs. Thatcher omits the crucial fact: much of the Global South was wealthier and more developed than Britain, France, or the Netherlands, often for centuries afterward. All then-rich developed nations were destroyed by cannons, drugs, fanaticism, and European ideologies (like "free markets" after actual free markets were dismantled), particularly by the British and their pirate enterprises (*privatizers*) like the East India Co. Tens of trillions were siphoned from India to England in just two centuries while hundreds of millions were massacred or deliberately starved. Russia achieved significant economic and social development until the Nazi barbarism (supported by Britain and America's great entrepreneurial successes) and was then harassed and blockaded during the Cold War by the same racist empires like hers.

The Congo, which Thatcher mentions, was repeatedly plundered and bled dry by Europeans until recently—with the natural collaboration of local collaborators. Not only did they steal trillions for the development of "free, intelligent, entrepreneurial nations," but within decades they exterminated ten million people and amputated the hands of thousands, if not millions, of other victims who didn't work fast enough for white entrepreneurial success.

Her indignation about environmental pollution in developing countries doesn't even warrant comment. A schoolchild knows better.

If the Northwest surpassed all other cultures—from Indigenous nations in America to ancient, highly productive Asian societies—it was through materialist fanaticism and the unrivaled development of instruments of war and destruction. Because their prosperity, as still understood today, is impossible without "destroying the competition." The Other who won't obey, the Other who isn't enslaved, colonized, or sycophantic, is always (always) a dangerous enemy.

It's no coincidence that when we speak of imperialism, we're accused of being "stuck in the sixties" or something similar—a tactic to silence the root of the problem which, like a root, remains strategically buried.

For further details, see *Flies in the Web: A History of the Commercialization of Existence—and Its Means* (there are better books, but this is the one I know best).

# MY WORTH EQUALS MY WEALTH

In late 2022, a Twitter feud went viral between former *kickboxer* and *influencer* Andrew Tate and young environmentalist Greta Thunberg. Tate, a far-right activist known for misogynistic statements, millionaire status, and anti-environmental stance, sent the following message to the Swedish teenager: *"Hello @gretathunberg. I own 33 cars. My Bugatti has a w16 8.0L turbo engine. My two Ferrari 812 competition models have 6.5L v12 engines. This is just the beginning. Send me your email address so I can provide a complete list of my car collection and their massive emissions."* The environmentalist responded with a fake email address (smalldickenergy@getalife.com), alluding to Tate's penis size—likely referencing the well-known complex of men who boast about large possessions. Tate's followers countered with arguments like *"And you, Greta, what do you have?"*

The controversy (which culminated in Tate's arrest and charges of human trafficking when his location in Romania was revealed through a pizza delivery video he himself posted featuring *Jerry's Pizza*) encapsulates our era. On one side, the patriarchal backlash against civil rights movements' achievements, stemming from frustration over lost privileges that fueled the new conservative and neofascist reaction. On the other, the climate catastrophe denialism born from consumerist culture that measures human worth by money and material possessions.

This culture, deeply rooted in our time, represents the culmination of life's commercialization that began with Capitalism itself (In later chapters, we'll examine this effect and practice in media). The same culture that reduces all human meaning to wealth is a trademark of new commercial artists—rappers, for instance, famous not only for tattooing their ideas on their skin but for boasting in their songs and throughout their lives about all the money they possess and all the women who throw themselves at them to get a share of that legitimately earned money. This phenomenon also bears the mark of the CIA and NSA when they invest millions in culture. What better way to neutralize critical art, problematic art, true art than by replacing it with submission to the god of money and obedience to a system that's logical for a tiny minority but absurd for the rest of society?

We've already outlined the process that led us to this proud zombie existence. After feudal systems were toppled in Europe and any other systems in plundered, brutalized colonies, *the market became identified with capitalism*, despite markets having existed for millennia while capitalism emerged mere centuries ago. Capitalism didn't invent markets or their rules; it simply turned their natural profit-seeking tendency into the center of human life, and wealth accumulation—whether through trade or massive imperialist plunder—into its functional and ideological objective. More than that: it turned individuals into producers and consumers, and human existence into a product. It commodified colonial inhabitants, first as race-based slaves, then as wage and class-based slaves.

Now, though overrepresented, inferior beings are no longer necessarily Black or mixed-race like Mr. Tate, but poor or property-less idealists without major capital, like Ms. Thunberg. That is, rich vs. poor, successful vs. failures, hard workers vs. lazy bums. A perfect class struggle that refuses to acknowledge class struggle. As historian Ellen Meiksins Wood observed, the capitalist market isn't a marketplace of opportunities but of imposition. The capitalist revolution lies not in markets but in the institutions (political, legal, cultural and ideological) that made them the center of human existence.

Capitalism was born from new forms of property ownership in the English countryside. By then, the millennia-old market had already begun a precapitalist process with the growth of cities in Italy and the Netherlands, but it became what historians call a "failed process." It was in rural England where the market freed itself from other social constraints and became an imposition and an outright dispossession—not just of land but of the psychological stability of the new tenant farmers. A Belgian veterinarian had observed that *"the English value their land only to profit from it."* On December 26, 1822, the Mexican ambassador in Washington, José Manuel Bermúdez Zozaya, reported to Foreign Minister José Manuel de Herrera: *"The arrogance of these republicans prevents them from seeing us as equals but rather as inferiors...; they deeply love our money, not us, nor are they capable of entering into agreements of alliance or trade except for their own convenience, disregarding reciprocity..."* Eleven years later, on June 10, a member of Parliament, Rigby Watson, explained the logic behind abolishing slavery and promoting consumerism among Black people: *"To make them work and cultivate in them a taste for luxuries and comforts, they must first be taught, little by little, to desire those objects attainable through labor. There is a progression from possessing necessities to desiring luxuries; once these luxuries are attained, they will become necessities across all social classes. This is the kind of progress through which the Blacks must pass, and this is the kind of education to which they must be subjected."* To cite just a few examples.

When human life was commercialized. After the great exception of the European Middle Ages, which lasted half a millennium, there came a moment when urban life (burgs) became separated from food production. Then, the market began imposing its rules on the rest of human existence (let alone the ecosystem and the rest of life on the planet). What Marx called the *"fetishism of commodities."* Later, the worker's labor became independent (or "alienated," in Marx's terms) from the final consumer product. In the 20th century, there was another moment when capital began to detach itself from production and consumption goods. In other words, it was a progressive and sustained process of *abstraction*, as noted by Ernesto Sábato seventy years ago in *Men and Gears*(1951), recalling the Russian thinker Nikolai Berdyaev: the Renaissance *"was a humanist movement that ended in dehumanization."*

# The Fourth Power of Power

Just a few miles from where I waste my life trying to understand the absurdity of our human species, Donald Trump has once again accused Mexico of abusing "the kindness of the United States" and China of "abusing the Panama Canal." Like in the 19th century, he also wants Canada as a state, but more amiably. After all, its inhabitants belong to a superior race.

China's abuse of the Panama Canal refers to it doing too much business with the West and, worse yet, with Latin America, our Backyard, our banana republics where people speak "the language of cleaning ladies." As President Ulysses Grant said in 1873, and as the British always practiced, *"once we have obtained all that protectionism can offer, we will also adopt free trade."*

Of course, more important than capitalism's ideological flexibility is its moral flexibility. Empires have always presented themselves as victims or with some divine right. When in 1832 Andrew Jackson, in his speech to Congress, justified the removal of Native peoples, he proclaimed: *"they attacked us without provocation."* We had to defend ourselves. From 1763 to today, the tradition has been to force Natives to sign treaties that would later be violated by the owners of the cannon whenever the treaties limited business opportunities by dispossessing "the inferior races." The same happened with the Treaty of Guadalupe Hidalgo in 1848, which forced Mexico to cede half its territory to the United States for a pittance and was never honored in the agreements protecting the rights of Mexicans left on this side of the new border. Like the lament of "The White Man's Burden," coined by British poet Rudyard Kipling and promoted by

Teddy Roosevelt, about the humanity of invaders in lands of "peaceful Blacks," that "perfectly stupid race," according to Roosevelt himself.

Now, what has always been the role of the mainstream press?

In January 2025, CNN—the supposedly anti-Trump network—pondered his expansionist proposals: *"Trump, in his own way, is addressing national security issues the U.S. must confront in a new world shaped by China's rise (...) Trump's musings about terminating the Panama Canal Treaty reflect concerns over foreign powers encroaching on the Western Hemisphere. This is not a new worry: it has been a recurring theme in history, from the Monroe Doctrine of 1823 when European colonialists were the threat. The issue persisted through Cold War fears of communism. Today's usurpers are China, Russia, and Iran."*

For Latin America, the actual usurpers—not in rhetoric but in practice—have always been the United States. It was a journalist, John O'Sullivan, who created the myth of Manifest Destiny. In 1852 he wrote: *"This continent and its adjacent islands belong to the whites; Blacks must remain slaves..."*

If we skip over three thousand U.S. interventions in the next fifty years, we might recall that, by capitalist logic, the Panama Canal never belonged to the U.S. any more than Manhattan's Hudson Yards belongs to Qatar, or the One World Trade Center and the new Waldorf Astoria in New York—or the mega-developments in Chicago and Los Angeles—belong to China, to name just a few recent examples.

Now, from both a moral standpoint and under international law, we could remember that Theodore Roosevelt stole Panama from Colombia through a Washington-funded revolution. The canal was built with the blood of hundreds of Panamanians forgotten by historical racism, just as it forgot the Chinese immigrants who built the railroads on the West Coast and the Irish on the East Coast—groups persecuted and killed for belonging to "inferior races."

If Washington paid even minimal compensation for all its invasions of Latin American countries since the 19th century, for all the democracies it destroyed, for all the bloody dictatorships imposed by cannon fire, for the "dollar diplomacy" or the CIA's Cold War sabotage campaigns (and beyond), the U.S. Treasury's gold reserves wouldn't cover a fraction of it. This says nothing of imperial crimes—often in collaboration with European empires (the supposed Monroe Doctrine adversaries) in Asia and Africa—which not only assassinated independence leaders like Patrice Lumumba but left oceans of death and destruction, all in the name of a democracy and freedom that never arrived and never mattered to the imperial lords of power.

The slave system that wrested Texas, New Mexico, Colorado, Arizona, Nevada, and California from Mexico didn't disappear with the Civil War. It merely changed names (sometimes not even that) to keep doing the same thing—just like the slaveholding banks and corporations: JP Morgan, Wells Fargo, Bank of America, Aetna, CSX Corporation, among others. In 1865, shackled slaves became wage slaves (in many cases not even that, working for tips like waitresses today), and just as during slavery, the system continued to be called *democracy*, while its constitutions (1789's and the Confederacy's 1861 version) protected "freedom of speech."

Now, as we formulated in $P = d.t$, the West will ramp up censorship of critics for the simple reason that its power is waning—and so is its tolerance. Since classical Greece, free speech has been a luxury of empires that feel threatened by no criticism. On the contrary:

it serves as decoration for their pretensions of freedom and democracy.

The dominant media have an abysmal record of complicity, always in freedom's name. When James Polk manufactured an excuse to invade Mexico and steal over half its territory, he staged a false flag attack. It was time to *"extend freedom to other territories,"* said Polk—meaning the reintroduction of slavery to a country that had outlawed it. His own soldiers and generals on campaign—Ulysses Grant, Zachary Taylor, and Winfield Scott—wrote that they had no right to be on Mexican soil. General Ethan Allen Hitchcock wrote in his diary: *"To tell the truth, we have no right to be here. It rather seems that the government has sent us with so few men to provoke the Mexicans and thus have a pretext for a war that would allow us to take California."*

The new mass press of that time, thanks to the invention of the rotary press, became the primary instrument of propaganda and "fake news" that sent thousands of volunteers to invade Mexico and, as reported by American generals, to kill, steal, and *"rape women in front of their own children and husbands."* America was not sending its best citizens.

When Polk learned of a minor incident on Mexican territory, he rushed to Congress and reported: the invader *"has shed American blood on American soil."* John Quincy Adams and others accused him of having manufactured an excuse for war against a country that was not materially prepared to defend itself. Abraham Lincoln also opposed this war (which Ulysses Grant would later call 'the wicked war') and had to withdraw from politics for years, as nothing silences moral shortcomings more effectively than blind patriotism.

Exactly the same thing happened over the next 150 years. It happened with the invented myth of *the Maine*, propagated by the yellow press of New York, led by Joseph Pulitzer and William Hearst, one of the media and film moguls. Hearst defended Hitler while accusing F.D. Roosevelt of being a communist. At the time, the mainstream press portrayed Hitler as a patriot, just as it now presents Netanyahu as an envoy of God.

The same happened with the most decorated American general of his generation, Smedley Butler, when in 1933 he dared to say: *"The flag follows the dollar and the soldiers follow the flag. I wouldn't go to war again to protect the investments of bankers... Our wars have been very carefully planned by nationalist capitalism. I served in the Marines for 33 years, and during most of that time, I was the muscle for Wall Street and big business... In short, I was a racketeer for capitalism..."*

When Butler began speaking his mind, he wasn't imprisoned for thought crimes, as was the case with socialist candidate Eugene Debs for opposing World War I. Instead, a more common tactic was used: the military hero was discredited as someone with psychological issues.

The same pattern continued for generations. The atomic bombs dropped on Japan, the massive aerial bombing of Korea, the use of chemical weapons in Vietnam. Lyndon Johnson invested millions of dollars in the press to support the Vietnam War and its genocide through massive bombings and chemical weapons used against civilians.

By then, the CIA's Operation Mockingbird had already injected all major Latin American newspapers with 'fake news' and editorials written in Miami and New York. It did the same with major U.S. media outlets, books, films, etc. The ideological police served corporate interests while leaving hundreds of thousands massacred in Central America alone—all in the name of 'national security' that produced strategic insecurity.

Before the massive 2003 invasion of Iraq—which left a million dead, millions displaced, and the entire Middle East in chaos—we published in marginal countries' newspapers about the illogic of the narrative justifying it. But the mainstream media succeeded in convincing Americans that the drums of war spoke truth. The New York Times took a stand in favor of the invasion as a patriotic act and 'national security.' In the name of patriotism, critics were censored by law (*Patriot Act*) and social harassment. The media couldn't even show images of soldiers returning in caskets. Much less the hundreds of thousands of massacred Iraqi civilians who never mattered in this collective cowardice that only brought profits to the usual super-rich merchants of death.

Years later, even when George Bush and his puppet, Spanish Prime Minister José María Aznar, admitted that the reasons for the invasion were false—that Saddam Hussein had no weapons of mass destruction (supplied by Germany and the U.S. in the '80s) nor ties to Al Qaeda (like the Taliban, the CIA's estranged offspring)—most Fox News consumers still believed the lie debunked by its own perpetrators. After all, they were trained to believe against all evidence.

In politics, narrative and reality are more divorced than in a J.K. Rowling novel. While major media outlets sell themselves as independent guardians of democracy, they are neither independent nor democratic. They depend not only on a handful of millionaire advertisers; the billions of dollars that corporations and lunatics like Elon Musk donate to political parties are the perfect business: *with every dollar they simultaneously buy both politicians and the media that promotes them*. The media are part of this plutocratic dictatorship, and their job (no different from priests delivering sermons in churches and cathedrals funded by nobility) is to invent an alternative reality complicit with the power of money, imperialism, and racism. All in the name of democracy, international law, and diversity.

Do you think this country needs more sycophants or more critics? Of course, everyone claims to want critics, but in silent practice all know that if someone wants to climb the ladder of success and power, sycophancy pays far better. This is known equally by poor immigrants, servile academics, lobby-bought politicians, and board members aspiring to become CEOs.

We're in the same situation as the 19th century: geopolitical expansion and racist arrogance. The difference is that back then, the United States was a rising empire, while today it's in decline. As European examples show, imperialisms have always been costly for their citizens, since they can't exist without permanent wars, but during their peaks they always generated profits—especially for those at the top. The problem arises with a declining empire. Then arrogance becomes extremely expensive and can only accelerate its decay, misery, and conflicts both within and beyond its borders.

Knowing how to negotiate in a world that doesn't belong to us, making friends rather than enemies, is the cheapest, most effective, fairest and most reasonable strategy. What more? The problem is that leading peace has always been harder than leading war—that failproof recourse of mediocrities, even when dragging their own country to destruction.

With each passing year we confirm history's march toward the fascism of last century's decaying empires. The first to fall will be the critics. When the ashes aren't from some poor defenseless country on the other side of the world but from the empire's very heart, survivors will deny three times over having participated in such cowardly arrogance.

As always, it will be too late, because if humanity has held truth and justice as supreme values, it has rarely practiced them. The norm has been the opposite.

# POSTCAPITALISM

# HUMAN SACRIFICES AND THE POLITICS OF CRUELTY

Throughout the millennial history of American peoples, we observe that the most peaceful and democratic societies, nations, and republics showed far greater social and gender equity than those distinguished by violence, hierarchy, and patriarchal dominance. The Incas and Aztecs were more violent and patriarchal than other available examples. On one hand, production surplus was accumulated by dominant elites through their armies. The Aztec god Huitzilopochtli—god of war who replaced female deities in their pantheon—after promising them already-inhabited lands, demanded human sacrifice rituals serving the political and imperial function of intimidating both subjects and outsiders. (*1)

On the other hand, we remember that across cultures, violence and war—from ritual sacrifices to male initiation into war culture and violence as masculinity symbols—were directly tied to intra-social domination through threat and fear instilled against the "foreigner," the enemy.

When modern empires emerged, as with the recent case of the United States in the late 19th century, consensus held that anti-imperialists were effeminate cowards, while imperialists were masculine, violent, and always ready to start some war. *"I am in favor of almost any war, and I believe this country needs one,"* said Theodore Roosevelt, while President McKinley faced sexuality accusations for refusing to start one against Spain. (*2)

War, a violent class and culture serve the function of dominating the societies that sustain them, perpetuating the power of an elite that disproportionately benefits from the very society it claims to defend and protect. No different from what occurs today.

Human sacrifice rituals are typically attributed to the Aztecs and other earlier Mesoamerican peoples—not without irony or outrage from conquistadors who exercised several times greater violence while "civilized" Europe was immersed in its own religious rituals of torture and extermination, such as forced conversion, the Inquisition, Christian-on-Christian massacres, and public torture/executions of poor thieves. Mesoamerican sacrifices were labeled as barbarism and fanaticism, ignoring the barbarism and fanaticism of the new capitalist Europe that massacred infinitely more lives worldwide based on the fanaticism of money—something even harder to justify than human sacrifice in the name of some distant god.

In a way, human sacrifices were replaced by more abstract and symbolic rituals—first animal sacrifices, then offerings. Yet this prehistoric/historic trait embedded in humanity's genetic code didn't disappear; it transformed. Today we see fascisms and wars of extermination, motivated not just by material interests but tolerated/justified even by those who don't directly benefit—reproducing the ancient ritual of sacrificing minorities to exercise violent, often genocidal energy. This genetic code buried deep in every human (more pronounced in some than others) particularly shines when individuals merge into a horde, an urban tribe, a social sect, a political party.

As elaborated in *Flies in the Spiderweb* (2023), the commercialization of existence turned ancestral strengths (attention to negative events, consumption of stimulants/calories) into *modern weaknesses*. Likewise, violence toward others is as ancient as solidarity—but the former reflects individual selfish survival, while the latter enabled societal survival as a foundational condition of civilizations.

The idea of freedom is ancient but almost never considered "equal-freedom"—liberty exercised through others' rights. It was always the freedom of the powerful: nobles, slavers, capitalists to decide for "inferior beings," vassals, shackled slaves, wage slaves. The "equal freedom" concept emerged among early persecuted Christians (not persecutors) but crystallized during Europe's Enlightenment—both from humanists and the conquistadors' profound encounter with Native Americans' more democratic, free, egalitarian world. By the early 16th century (especially early 18th century), Indigenous American ideas of "equal freedom" (social/sexual/racial) and their ancient democratic practices became conscious in Europe, centralizing intellectual debate and later popular movements.

According to Rousseau and his contemporary followers, agriculture's invention—particularly its creation of food surplus—ended egalitarian societies. Disputes over managing this surplus birthed not just early state forms but social classes.

To this we must add nationalist religions' creation—more violent ideologies imposed upon larger groups through effective coercion via shared concepts of *being* and *oughtness*, enforced through fear, ritual, psychological terrorism, and duty beyond one's own life.

But Europe's discovery of America inspired not just these utopian/anti-European ideas among Enlightenment philosophers, nor merely the idealistic creation of the United States (in open contradiction with its reality of exploitation/oppression/inequality), nor solely utopian and later scientific socialists—it provided a living counterexample to Rousseau's theory about primitive egalitarian hunter societies transitioning into hierarchical agricultural ones. In the native nations of America, we find agricultural societies with highly sophisticated systems—some even more developed than Europe's—where private property beyond personal use was unknown, especially regarding land which was worked communally. These were far more egalitarian societies with nature-based religious systems less cohesive and fanatical than Europe's, and with clearly more democratic political systems.

The fear of losing private land ownership and slaves in ancient Rome led to a sharp increase in punitive forces (nonexistent in complex Native American societies), such as police and armies, and simultaneously to the desire (and necessity) for theft. Not without paradox, violence and repression were supported and promoted in the name of freedom, because they were tied to the power of private property held by a minority.

Capitalism, and especially post-capitalism, has discovered the philosopher's stone capable of magically translating the power of capital into political, social, cultural, and religious power. This act of magic is also addictive and practiced by only one psychological type among hundreds of other human characteristics and abilities: the obsession with accumulating money, the skill to amass it, and the insensitivity toward any possible negative effects of this addiction on the rest of humanity. In other words, the ideal prototype of the successful billionaire capable of buying entire governments is someone obsessed with economic gains—a radically simplified, one-dimensional individual. What psychological profile fits perfectly with this functional demand for cruelty, for the ritual of human sacrifice?

One defining aspect of psychopaths lies in their inability to feel compassion, empathy, or the slightest reflection of others' pain as their own. This emotional deficiency—which normally explains the survival of both human and animal species—leads them to the opposite. Among the few sources of pleasure they can access to relieve their insensate lives are sex (or its substitutes) and delight in others' suffering.

We're shocked to see how a president, prime minister, senator, or successful businessman can make decisions causing thousands— if not millions—of people pain with seductive conviction. Typically, they excuse themselves with something abstract and arbitrary like '*efficiency*', twisting the meaning of values and emotions defined simply and understandably for millennia—such as compassion and solidarity.

A contemporary example is the many social leaders elevated by capitalist systems for their high functionality. Writer Ayn Rand spearheaded the reaction against the moral victory of World War II that defeated—militarily and culturally—the West's fascist sadism. In 2024, Argentina's President Milei declared in Washington that "social justice is violent." A decades-old outburst repackaged in digestible pills against any form of social sensibility, echoing Ryan Ann's mantra from 60 years prior: "*evil is compassion, not selfishness.*"

We shouldn't be surprised by policies of cruelty or attempt to justify them outside capitalism and beyond humanity's oldest psychopathic psychology and human sacrifice rituals: *others' suffering isn't collateral damage* from "necessary measures"—it serves social control functions and provides pleasure to psychopaths and the collective ego that will never acknowledge it, not even in a mirror. There's no need to humanize these *successful individuals* by understanding them, just as we needn't comprehend why someone might rape then murder. Not even novelists must attempt to feel what criminals feel. Simply noting the facts suffices.

Ideas of equal freedom and democracy, though ancient traditions in America, remain recent in human evolution. Neurologically speaking, they're fragile—constantly harassed and threatened by the reptilian core of our most primitive cortices, beyond the human brain's frontal lobe. All that capitalism doesn't restrain but rather reproduces, multiplies, and concentrates without a trace of human emotion—like robots, like Javier Milei, Donald Trump, or Elon Musk—like capital itself.

# Superior Culture—That of the Leader or the Thug?

On March 4, 2025, in a speech at the University of Austin, Palantir's billionaire CEO Alex Karp delivered a 19th-century classic: *"I don't believe all cultures are equal... What I'm saying is that this nation* [the United States] *is incredibly special and we shouldn't see it as equal, but as superior"*. As detailed in the book *Plutocracy: Tyrannosaurs of the Anthropocene* (2024) and various television programs, Karp belongs to Silicon Valley's sect that—with CIA support and Wall Street's corporate oligarchy—promotes replacing inefficient liberal democracy with corporate monarchy.

Now, our nation, our culture—superior in what way? In efficiency for invading, enslaving, oppressing other peoples? Superior in fanaticism and arrogance? Superior in the historical psychopathology of tribes believing themselves chosen by their own gods (what a coincidence) which, far from implying solidarity responsibility toward "inferior peoples," automatically becomes license to kill, steal, and exterminate others? Isn't Anglo-Saxon colonization of Asia, Africa, and America's history one of land dispossession, wealth theft, and obsessive exploitation of human beings (Indigenous, African, mixed-race, poor whites) seen as capitalization tools rather than people? What are we discussing when invoking "superior culture" with such indiscriminate claims carrying hidden yet potent religious mysticism—like Manifest Destiny?

We've not only addressed this in newspapers a quarter-century ago but warned then about the fascism that would suicide this proud West now complaining enemies are destroying it, as Elon Musk declared days earlier. One such extensive essay—written in 2002, published by Uruguay's *La República* in January 2003 and New York's *Monthly Review* in 2006—was titled "The Slow Suicide of the West."

This ideology of selfishness and the alienated individual as supreme ideals, promoted since Adam Smith in the 18th century and radicalized by writers like Ayn Rand and presidents ranging from world powers like Donald Trump to neocolonial puppets like Javier Milei, has revealed itself for what it is: pure and hardcore supremacism, pure and brutal cannibalistic pathology. Both racism and imperialist patriotism are expressions of tribal egomania, disguised as their opposites: love and the species' survival instinct.

To give it a veneer of intellectual justification, the ideologues of 21st-century fascist right-wingers resort to zoological metaphors like the Alpha Male. This image is based on steppe wolf packs where a small group follows a male who will save them from cold and hunger. An epic image that seduces millionaires who've never experienced hunger or cold. For others who aren't millionaires but see themselves as threatened from below (see "The Paradox of Social Classes"), the Alpha Male represents the ideological translation of a historical privileged class's catharsis—those who see their special rights losing the adjective *special* and becoming simply *rights*, a bare noun. That is, they react furiously to the potential loss of special rights based on gender, class, race, citizenship, culture, or hegemony. All these special rights justified as in the 19th century: we have the right to enslave Black people and plunder our colonies because we're a superior race, a superior culture, and therefore God loves us and hates our enemies, whom we must exterminate before they get the same idea—but without our good arguments.

Ironically, the idea of being "God's chosen" or nature's favorites doesn't drive fanatics to care for "inferior humans" as they do their pets—quite the opposite: the fate of inferiors and the weak must be enslavement, obedience, or extermination. If they defend themselves, they're terrorists.

The latest version of these supremacisms—which commit genocide in Palestine or the Congo with fanatical pride and conviction while demonizing women in the U.S. demanding equal rights—recently found its *catch-all metaphor* in the image of the steppe wolf's Alpha Male. However, if we pay attention to the behavior of these animals and other species, we'll see a much more complex and contradictory reality.

Frans de Waal, professor at Emory University and for decades one of the most renowned experts in chimpanzee studies, made it his mission to demolish this fantasy. The idea of the *alpha male* stems from 1940s wolf studies, but—not without irony—de Waal himself lamented that an American politician (ultraconservative House Speaker Newt Gingrich) popularized his book *Chimpanzee Politics* (1982) and the alpha male concept for all the wrong reasons.

Alpha males aren't *bullies*, but conciliatory leaders. "*Alpha males among chimpanzees are popular if they maintain peace and bring harmony to the group.*" When a true leader falls ill (as in the case of chimpanzee Amos), they aren't sacrificed—the group takes care of them.

According to de Waal, "*we must distinguish between dominance and leadership. There are males who may be the dominant force, but those males end up badly in the sense that they're expelled or killed... Then there are males with leadership qualities, who break up fights, defend the vulnerable, comfort the distressed. If you have that kind of alpha male, the group rallies around him and allows him to remain in power for a long time.*" This period usually lasts four years, though there are records of alpha males leading for 12 years—those who typically distributed food and maintained political alliances with younger leaders.

According to de Waal, an alpha leader will be judged by their ability to resolve conflicts and establish peaceful order for their society.

During conflicts, alpha leaders *"don't take sides with their best friend; they avoid or resolve fights and generally defend the most vulnerable. This makes them extremely popular within the group because they provide security for lower-ranking members."*

The alpha male leads by having the support of most females and some males, but other young males will always use the same strategy to dethrone him and impose dominance: first they begin with indirect, distant provocations to test the leader's reaction. If there's no response, the strongest young male will try to recruit others to escalate provocations that gradually gain ground and grow more violent. Then he secures allies through favors. Though the *alpha bully* candidate cares nothing for infants—only power—he attempts to appear affectionate with various females' offspring, exactly like politicians on the campaign trail.

## BIOLOGY AND TRADITIONAL VALUES

On August 27, 2024, Argentina's Minister of Justice, Mariano Cúneo Libarona, addressed the Congressional Women's Commission. Justifying the cancellation of gender violence programs, he declared in a tone reminiscent of military dictatorships from decades past:

*"Gender is over—our value is family. What are traditional family values? Love, unity, work, education, solidarity, equality. Equality before the law. Equal treatment."*

A clear example of linguistic appropriation, the same tactic used by 19th-century slaveholders, 20th-century neoliberals, and 21st-century libertarians against one of their greatest victims: the (ideolexical) word freedom. Aren't love, unity, work, education, solidarity, equality, equality before the law, and equal treatment fundamental values for those fighting for rights unrecognized or denied by fanatics of 'traditional family values'?

After this arbitrary and arrogant seizure of values cherished by marginalized groups, the minister grew more specific—and honest: *"We reject diversity of sexual identities*[sic]*, which doesn't align with biology... Yes."* Here he received applause from his party's representatives—the ruling party.

The minister displayed not just authoritarianism and arbitrariness, but also ignorance—three traditional values currently fashionable among reactionaries drunk on media and political power.

In February 2010, in an article titled "The Morality of Dogs" published in Mexico's *Milenio*, we responded to Archbishop Antonio Chedraui who had declared on Mexican television that *"The abnormal cannot be normal.*" After this commendable tautology, he posed his rhetorical question:

"*Have you ever seen an animal, a dog having sexual relations with another dog of the same sex?*" he said, just before a bark was heard.

Well, homosexuality isn't rare in nature (not to mention interspecies sexual relations). In fact, it's part of species' evolutionary advantage, especially among humans.

Fourteen years later, we're back with the same mediocre and ignorant arguments, based on male insecurity and other personal and collective phobias.

Mr. Justice Minister of Argentina:

If there's anything that doesn't align with biology, it's what people like you call "traditional values"—things like celibacy and monogamy. Furthermore, Mr. Minister, if you knew anything about biology (we're all ignorant, but some flaunt it), you'd be scandalized by nature's sexual diversity. It's precisely diversity (largely produced by the emergence of sex on this planet) that allows a species to survive and *evolve*—something else that has never pleased the fanatics in your club.

Diversity isn't just crucial in biology and ecosystems, but in human cultures too. Even in science: any halfway decent academic knows that science, including biology, has advanced (or evolved) by not just tolerating but promoting diversity of theories, viewpoints, and radical criticism, to distinguish truth from falsehood, to stop wasting time with ignoramuses like you who recall the days of the Holy Inquisition (champions of traditional values, no doubt), which not only censored Galileo Galilei for stating something outside religious dogma but also persecuted, tortured, and burned thousands of people in civilized Europe, especially those who didn't align with "traditional values."

Even the military dictatorships of the continent, like your country's, repeated their defense of freedom, patriotism, and traditional family values while torturing prisoners with electric cattle prods applied to their bound genitals. This sadistic obsession with torture and moral humiliation replicated the Holy Inquisition's practices, like the *Judas' chair* (a historical fact always questioned by some Catholics), which was nothing more than a pyramid seat where heresy suspects were slowly impaled until their anuses or vaginas were destroyed.

All in the name of God, civilization, family, and traditional family values—needless to say.

# AUGUSTUS TRUMP

A generation before Christ, Augustus ended the Roman Republic by appealing to religion, presenting himself as Apollo's favorite, subjugating the senate, and becoming Rome's first emperor. He promoted upper-class fertility, traditionalist moralism, and patriotic literature like Virgil's *Aeneid*—commissioned propaganda about Rome's fictional past glory.

Augustus capitalized on social instability with charismatic, demagogic rhetoric about *making Rome great again* under the Golden Eagle symbol. Five centuries later, Augustulus became the Western Empire's last emperor, defeated by Germanic barbarians.

The American Empire, humanity's most powerful, will likely also be history's briefest. It's held that title for one-tenth of Rome's European duration and one-hundredth of Byzantium's.

Meanwhile, China will end that historical anomaly called the "Century of Humiliation" and regain its millennia-old status as the top economic power. We hope China's lessons from those hundred years won't turn it into a Franco-Anglo-Saxon-style empire but rather preserve its ancient tradition of not subjugating peoples across the planet.

Trump may well be both Augustus and Augustulus simultaneously. We might hope that this hegemonic transition avoids the violent Thucydides' Trap, as did the handover from Britain to the United States, but in that case there was strategic continuity within Anglo-Saxon capitalism. Hegemony simply passed between allies.

Now the differences are substantial, and above all, the Anglo-Saxon obsession with preventing any global competition promises major conflict. The Northwest finds itself confronting not just a new success story—communist China—but also its own domestic poverty and international decline. No longer just exporting violence as it historically has, it now consumes violence internally. As solution, it resorts to its customary religious-style narratives that deny all contradictory evidence.

One of its most recent sermons has been justifying Chinese socialism's success by equating it with American state capitalism—despite Chinese corporations remaining subordinate to the communist government while Western corporations dominate their states, and despite China's economy being government-planned rather than corporate-directed. China has a market economy (something capitalism didn't invent but constrained) yet isn't capitalist. It's a communist nation in a still-capitalist world.

Beyond material power, what truly worries the Northwest is what has driven it for generations: the need to abort any successful model that isn't "The Only Possible System"—corporate capitalism. *Anglo-Saxon success wasn't built on capitalism but on overseas imperialism.* The capitalist countries serving as colonial suppliers at starvation prices were more capitalist than the United States itself.

Now the Anglo-capitalist success story decays through lost global power and capitalism's inherent internal contradictions laid bare: nearly a million homeless in U.S. streets; epidemics of addiction and overdose deaths; periodic massacres; ethnic hatred masking ruthless class warfare; students debt-enslaved;*indenture* widening inequality; unstoppable criminality; ascendant fascism; the unthinkable admission that liberal democracy (plutocracy's political circus) no longer functions; recognition (now from both poor right-wingers and wealthy capitalists) that *democracy* never worked; that oligarchs have taken Washington unmasked to finish hijacking what was called democracy while investing their plunder in Armageddon wars...

Now, if the *success story* politics (the right, simplified) and narratives about *democracy* and *freedom* have entered panic and confessional catharsis, on the other side (the left), certain taboos and totems have shattered permanently. Suddenly millions of Americans acknowledge obvious truths like:

1. Patriotism is just another truth-suppressing blindfold over justice.

2. The problem isn't democracy but its substitute: global hijacking by Anglo-Saxon tech-financial oligarchy.

3. The neoliberal dogma that private corporations perform better and cheaper has failed.

4. The rampant criminality and corruption of shadow governments like NSA, CIA, Wall Street and Silicon Valley.

5. The shattered consensus about empire's benevolence. Before Marco Rubio's confirmation as Secretary of State, while being handcuffed in the Capitol, an activist shouted what millions think: "Rubio's bloodthirsty... just wants perpetual war; free Cuba from sanctions that kill people. Freedom for Palestine." Other veterans were arrested yelling at Blinken: "We need money here, not for bombing Gaza's children."

6. The wholesale purchase of politicians, senators and *representatives* by Washington's biggest lobbies. In January 2025, Senator Bernie Sanders, referring to Netanyahu and the Israeli lobby AIPAC, stated: "Most Americans don't want us supporting a government that kills children; but if you say that, you'll face AIPAC and other millionaires and you'll lose elections... Many senators tell me 'God, what Netanyahu's doing is monstrous, but I can't vote against it

because they'll destroy my political career.' They know that if corporations aren't pleased, they'll lose elections..."

None of these critiques and ideas are new. Many of us have been writing about this since the 90s. Not earlier because we hadn't been born yet. What's new is that simultaneously, as the fascist politics of the super-rich seize power in the White House—backed by a majority of the population consuming their products—a new and growing minority has come out of the closet with heightened awareness of the *de facto* class struggle.

On Monday the 20th, Donald Trump assumes power again. His stern face alone speaks volumes. Not even his followers are hopeful. As Jorge Luis Borges would say, *they are united not by love, but by horror.* As Italian journalist Oriana Fallaci wrote in 2001—and we criticized as the dawn of a dangerous era ("The Slow Suicide of the West" 2002)—they are united by "rage and pride."

Now, we also shouldn't overlook that the more nationalist, fascist, and feudal-capitalist right advances, the more evident becomes a rupture driving people toward the left—as always—but now, for the first time in a century, in radical ways.

# Against The Dehumanization Of Poor Immigrants

The fight for immigrants' rights is the fight for Human Rights—that increasingly evident irrelevance when they don't serve powerful interests. But immigration isn't just a right; it's also the consequence of a global system violently discriminating between rich and poor, capitalists and workers. This age-old class struggle isn't just obscured through cultural, ethnic, and sexual wars—as occurred for centuries with racial and religious conflicts—but through the very demonization of the concept "class struggle," practiced by the rich and powerful while attributed to leftist ideologues as some evil project. Class struggle—the violent dispossession and dictatorship of the ultra-wealthy over working classes—is observable through any quantitative measurement.

This culture of barbarism and humiliation, of cruel politics and selfish ethics, occurs within every nation and replicates globally—from imperial nations to their servile capitalist colonies and their exceptions: the blockaded, demonized rebel alternatives.

Immigration illegality was invented over a century ago to extend the illegality of imperial invasions against weaker nations. It was invented to prevent the consequences of colonized peoples' exploitation—maintained in servitude through cannon fire, systematic massacres, strategic eternal debts still bleeding them dry today, and secret agencies that assassinated, manipulated media, destroyed democracies, toppled rebellious dictatorships, plunged half the world into chaos, and dehumanized slaves from day one—some of them happy slaves.

Illegal immigration didn't just punish the disinherited of this historical process but also those persecuted by the multiple brutal dictatorships Europe and the U.S. spread across Africa and Latin America—with various terrorist groups designed in Washington, London, and Paris: the Contras in Central America, Death Squads in South America, extermination plans like Operation Condor, the *Organisation armée secrète* in Africa, Islamic terrorists like Al Qaeda, the Taliban, ISIS—all created by the CIA and its accomplice mafias to crush independent, secular, and socialist projects in Africa and the Middle East... Meaning it's not just colonial capitalism expelling its own people, but the root of that brutality: imperial capitalism.

Then the victims become criminals. As happened when Haiti dared declare itself free and independent in 1804, as with other slave abolition cases: slaveowners demanded government compensation for losing their private property of flesh and blood. Not the victims who built America's wealth, banks, corporations; not the slaves who built the White House and Capitol building. In the same way, according to Trump and his supremacist horde, the Panama Canal belongs to the invading master and not to the Panamanians and Caribbeans who lost thousands of lives in its construction.

Immigration in almost all its forms, from economic to political, is a direct consequence of these historical injustices. The rich do not emigrate; they dominate their countries' economies and media, then send their "profits" to tax havens or as investments that sustain the global slavery system under the guise of "high-risk" ventures.

The rich are guaranteed entry to any country. The poor, on the other hand, are treated as suspects from the moment they approach an embassy of any powerful nation. Typically, their applications are denied, forcing them to take on $15,000 loans from coyotes just to enter a country that prints the global reserve currency—only to work for years as slaves while being doubly criminalized. They aren't playing victims, as some assimilated academics claim. They are actual victims. They are wage slaves (often not even that) under constant psychological terrorism endured by both them and their children. In the United States, hundreds of thousands of children don't regularly attend school because they work under slave conditions, no different from the indentured *indenture* slaves of centuries past.

For decades, every year, illegal immigrants contribute one hundred billion dollars to the Social Security funds of complaining voters—money they'll never receive, but which goes to those who spend their days lamenting the jobs "stolen" by immigrants. As if this scale of injustice weren't enough, eventually the most devoted, persecuted, and impoverished workers are thrown into prisons as terrorists and deported in chains and humiliation—ironically by the cruelty of rulers condemned for serious crimes by their own country's justice system, as is the case with the current White House occupants. To this remarkable *cowardice* they call *courage*, just as they call *freedom* the *enslavement* of others and *victims* the world's *predators*.

To this we must add the traditional collaboration of promoted collaborators—from academics to voters, from journalists to *Latino*, *Indian*, or *African* members of imperial governments who, as a "solution to the immigration problem" and the sovereign disobedience of some Southern nations, impose more blockades and sanctions to further strangle their less successful brothers who chose not to emigrate to the Land of God. A pathology later sold as an example of "success based on merit and hard work." Because that is the only pleasure of psychopaths who cannot find happiness in anything: not their own success, but the defeat and humiliation of everyone else.

One of fascism's characteristics, aside from invoking a nonexistent past, is exploiting, persecuting, demonizing, blaming, and punishing all those without the economic or military power to defend themselves—as is the case with poor immigrants in the world's imperial centers.

We, stripped of the sectarian interests of global power and answering only to a sense of morality and Human Rights, raise our voices to protest against the world's largest organized crime syndicate, certain that this perversion of human cruelty will eventually collapse—not under its own weight, but through the courage and solidarity of those below.

# Racism and the Refugees of Hegemonic Capitalism

The refugee crises at the U.S. southern border are not the result of any external invasion threatening National Security. They aren't even the consequence of "Washington's soft policies," as politicians and major media in this country endlessly repeat. They are the outcome of intersecting contradictions within today's hegemonic capitalism.

On one hand, we have the law of supply and demand, and on the other, a long tradition of interventionism by the superpower that—since the 19th century, without respite and in the name of fighting corruption—has promoted corruption in "the chaotic black republics." In the name of freedom, democracy, peace, and human rights, it has imposed a prolific list of protectorates, civil-military dictatorships, paramilitary terrorism, and death squads—even in so-called democracies. The border crisis, as repeated and magnified by the press and politicians, is not a crisis for the United States. It is only a crisis for the poor and displaced by the very system of hegemonic capitalism that demonizes them.

To resolve capitalism's contradictions—the undesirable effects of the venerated Law of Supply and Demand—there are laws crafted by politicians serving corporations in the name of defending an entire nation. In this sense, all laws are anti-capitalist, as they contradict, limit, or prevent the immediate expression of supply (immigrant labor) and demand (national consumption). Here is where imperialism emerges to attempt resolving the contradictions of its own ideology, and beyond its laws, narratives appear about "our borders" that must be "defended from invasion" by the poor, alongside the altruistic "selfless struggle for freedom" through interventions beyond others' borders. In the fictitious freedom of the market, freedom is only accepted when those with power impose their freedom upon the liberated. For these same reasons, in countries like the United States, for over a century laws have been written by capitalist corporations to shield themselves from the unintended consequences of free market freedom—and above all, to protect themselves from the freedom of those below: the poor, the inferior races, the peripheral nations.

With the communist excuse exhausted (none of those "*shithole countries*" are communist but rather more capitalist than the U.S.), they revert to the racial and cultural excuses of the pre-Cold War era. In every dark-skinned worker, they see a criminal, a rapist—not a human being, not an opportunity for mutual development. Even immigration laws themselves fear poor workers. Anyone who has applied for a visa knows that before appearing at a U.S. embassy anywhere in the world, they must erase the word *work* from their personal vocabulary. One can be a perfect drone with money and boast about it—but never a poor worker.

While in the U.S., Social Security and public healthcare remain under media attack—subject to progressive defunding by governments aiming to transfer resources to the Pentagon and promote private health and security coverage—over 60,000 Americans die annually from drug addictions, mostly due to prescribed opioids. In 2017, according to the U.S. government's National Institute on Drug Abuse, 47,000 people died from opioid overdoses. The epidemic of this drug began in the 1990s when powerful pharmaceutical companies assured doctors their product wasn't addictive, despite studies contradicting this claim. The propaganda campaign to manipulate doctors closely resembled those invented by Edward

Bernays half a century earlier to sell cigarettes, eggs, bacon, and coups d'état.

But no one remembers anything. They only see a few thousand impoverished souls threatening to destroy the world's most powerful nation with their penises and vaginas. As the private prison industry (receiving millions in federal funds) flourishes along the southern border, illegal immigrants and legal refugees are criminalized for being poor and for the sin of not being Caucasian. The business, like any other, exists solely to increase its clientele. The problem is that here, the clients are poor men and women seeking a decent life, searching for a little peace and hard work—the only terrible thing they know how to do. Unless they're refugees. Since others' despair and self-righteous outrage is a business model, prison corporations inflate the days, weeks, and months that potential criminals—even children—must spend detained unnecessarily, violating international law while complying with the laws of the "nation of laws."

Since 1980, desperate emigration from the Northern Triangle has multiplied tenfold. Not because borders have opened or travel conditions improved—migrants still rely on their legs as primary transportation while borders have been exponentially militarized. The paramilitary terrorism funded by northern corporations, Washington's wars in the 1980s, and its 2.0 coups in the new century have produced immediate and lasting effects. By 2020, migrants fleeing violence and misery in Central America's ultra-capitalist neocolonial protectorates (Guatemala, El Salvador, and Honduras) will constitute nearly 90% of the total flow. Since communism can't be blamed (worse yet, only seven percent of migrants come from the "Nicaraguan regime") and the ultra-capitalist neo protectorates aren't blockaded countries, their sick culture gets blamed. When not directly blaming the cursed race. In response, Washington resists receiving these dangerous refugees, whether children or poor women. Not by mere accident, the superpower of compassionate Christians accepts a hundred times fewer refugees per thousand inhabitants than Lebanon, and even six times fewer than impoverished, blockaded Venezuela.

With no signs of change, politicians in the United States continue warning about the danger of terrorists among the poor seeking asylum. Nothing better than frightening the people with a nonexistent invasion to avoid discussing the violence and historical massacres by white supremacist terrorism. Nothing better than scaring the middle class with the threat of dark-skinned poor people to obscure how two men—Jeff Bezos and Elon Musk—now possess more wealth than forty percent of the superpower's population, while homelessness and the precarization of wage-slave labor continues growing. All this fuels the furious defense of the lower classes toward their upper-class benefactors with clichés like "the lazy want to invade us to live off government handouts," "the poor steal from me through taxes," and "the solution isn't taking from the rich but helping them prosper"—as if the wealthy hadn't already hijacked enough of history's progress and all the labor of those below who sustain and defend them like gods.

Racism, the business of exploiting those below, is neither created nor destroyed—it only transforms.

# SUCCESSFUL EXAMPLES OF FINANCIAL NEOCOLONIALISM

Based on the study we developed in *Flies in the Web*(2023), we can see that the particularity of the so-called Asian Tigers, including communist Vietnam (recurring examples in neoliberal propaganda by The One and its scribes), lies in their integration into a global financial system. All the theories, "explainer videos," and media sermons extolling these countries' miracles omit each part's role in the whole—each individual, each country in the current global system, which, as we've seen, differs little from the system inherited from previous centuries.

As seen in earlier chapters, global capitalism loves slaves—whether *chattel slaves*(shackled slaves), *indentures* (term slaves), or wage slaves (flexible human resources). The contemporary Asian Tigers are just four countries: two dedicated to finance due to their strategic geographic and transit positions and ideal time zones for the eternal continuity of global markets (Hong Kong and Singapore); the other two are manufacturing hubs (South Korea and Taiwan).

The first two are micro-republics that, like other micro or virtual republics, serve ultraliberal financial capitalism but have centralized governments playing decisive roles in economic processes. Beyond their notorious medieval laws, authoritarianism, and heavy intervention in macroeconomic design, Singapore's government owns 90 per cent of habitable areas and participates in over a third of the country's major corporations.

The same goes for the two manufacturing Tigers, with the particularity that Taiwan and South Korea are receptacles for technological investments. London and Wall Street need manufacturing slaves in countries without mineral reserves. In other words, they need these countries to have obsessive, enslaved production for electronics exports while maintaining above-average education—of course, a culture and education molded to utilitarianism, the commercialization of life, and above all, the interests of global financial centers.

The mass export of high-tech products (following massive capital investment and the reason for these neocolonies' "economic prosperity") offsets the mass import of these products by financial centers—i.e., consumer countries like Europe and especially the United States. If they had raw materials coveted by the core, as in Africa and Latin America, their education would be as depressed as their investments: history shows that the less educated the population in extractive countries, the cheaper the labor, the more authoritarian and classist their society, and the more obedient the masses suffering this condition for the benefit of local oligarchies and their partners—foreign capital and corporations.

The primary administrators of investments, money production, private and international banks, and the transfer of surpluses from productive countries to the hegemonic nation with history's largest deficit (the United States) continue residing in today's imperial centers—and above all, continue benefiting, before anyone else, The One, the international oligarchy, that minuscule club of men who dominate global finance and opinion—though never, of course, in absolute terms.

The remaining countries in the Global South are divided into two types of colonies: (1) strategically indebted economies with raw materials and (2) the world's factories with trade surpluses, lacking natural wealth but with abundant labor and high levels of utilitarian education—equally enslaved. To illustrate, one need only study living conditions for workers in Hong Kong or South Korea. Not even the UN Development Index can account for these qualitative factors, focusing instead on easily quantifiable metrics like education (without specifying what kind), health, and per capita income. China, due to its demographic particularity, has managed to position itself in a third category—neither a colony of the system nor yet the center of a financial empire benefiting from vampirizing the rest of the world, as has been capitalism's imperial history.

Before, industries were in imperial metropolises like London and New York. Now they reside in the "financial industry"—still in London and New York.

# WHY DOES ELON MUSK HATE WIKIPEDIA?

In 2008, Argentine philosopher Hugo Biagini published his *Dictionary of Alternative Thought*. Biagini often invited me to collaborate on his projects (like *Latin America Toward a Second Independence*, with Arturo Roig, 2007; or his *Dictionary of Intellectual Autobiographies*, 2019), and on that occasion my contribution was just one entry titled "The Disobedient Society." There, I reiterated a response to Wikipedia co-founder Larry Sanger, who abandoned the project in 2007, deeming it a failure due to its lack of authority. In 2020, Sanger accused Wikipedia of being dominated by "leftists"—a debatable claim. Less debatable is that those who love money won't dedicate their lives to teaching or Wikipedia.

To me, despite its flaws, Wikipedia represented a recent and successful example of knowledge organization independent of political or economic authority—a "form of cultural disobedience." In Biagini's *Dictionary*, I noted: "Contrary to predictions, the collaborative writing of information by millions of anonymous individuals worldwide has not resulted in chaos but in reliability (according to traditional studies) on par with the Encyclopædia Britannica (...) In the disobedient society, postindustrial education progressively replaces industrialist (standardizing) education, just as the latter replaced scholastic education during the Industrial Revolution. In the political sphere, one of its prerequisites is direct democracy (...) This diagnosis suggests that traditional representative systems (like parliamentary government) will lose their importance in societal decision-making, much as absolute monarchs once did in favor of parliaments. This very idea—of worsening conditions imposed by imperial power (here, the globalization of North American culture...)—may itself be a reaction by traditional powers against the rise of the disobedient society... Yet we might consider that the conflict stems not from disobedience's inevitable radicalization but from traditional powers' reaction to it." (506-508)

All this despite continuous pressure and interference from institutionalized mafias like the CIA (for which Elon Musk works as an agent with access to classified documents). Since Wikipedia's early years, edit wars have been traced to IP addresses originating from the CIA itself—before the NRL developed Tor, an anonymous browser that also slipped from their control (making it open-source was inevitable for true "untraceability"). Yet the CIA didn't reduce but increased its use of such tools. The same happened with Linux, as its founder acknowledged by denying it verbally while affirming it tacitly.

Wikipedia's other founder, Jimmy Wales, began from a libertarian and capitalist philosophy, but his project conflates right-wing anarchism (anti-government, like original Marxism) with left-wing anarchism (egalitarian). In 2005, I had already labeled the Libertarian Party as a "horde of lunatics."

Elon Musk has mocked Wikipedia's begging for survival, similar to the remaining public radio and television networks in the United States. NPR and PBS are hated by Musk, who wants to see them disappear. Due to progressive state defunding, these public networks have had to resort to donations.

Wales has insisted that Wikipedia's principle of not funding itself through advertising is to preserve its independence. Of course, when unrestricted, donations are a double-edged sword. This is where the dosage of medication makes an absolute difference between life and death. An obvious example was the abolition of donation caps for political parties in 2010, which recently allowed Musk to purchase his access to the White House with a *"donation"* of $250 million to Donald Trump's campaign.

Politicians, media, and public opinion can be bought. But some things cannot, like love and dignity. In Wikipedia's case, it's a thorn in the heel of ultra-billionaires like Musk: how is it possible that a global source of information exists that isn't traded on the London or New York Stock Exchange? If Musk could buy Twitter for $44 billion (without spending a dollar of his own money), change its name, and in the name of free speech begin manipulating the algorithm to censor and boost the global visibility of Trump and himself, how is it possible that Superman, with all his superpowers, can't write his own biography or the history of political, social, sexual, and racial ideas? What horror!

To make matters worse, English Wikipedia maintains a fact that wounds his naturally inflated ego: *"On the first anniversary of the acquisition* [of Twitter], *Musk declared the company's value at $19 billion, a 55 percent depreciation from the purchase price of $44 billion."*

If since the Middle Ages nobles donated to churches and cathedrals built by artisans, who would then go listen to sermons by priests living off donations from nobles and burghers, how is it possible that even in this current return to the Middle Ages, feudal lords can buy God but not a damn encyclopedia?

Musk offered a billion dollars for Wikipedia and proposed renaming it Wokepedia or Dickipedia (Cockipedia), confirming that the world's owners are neither happy nor capable of living at peace with themselves—let alone with the rest of humanity.

The White House commander-in-chief who came from South African apartheid knows Wikipedia is one of the rare examples of independence from big capital, which is why he can't stand the thought that something might exist without the possibility of being bought—that is, controlled by the psychopaths of global and class apartheid.

Just like his father's fortune, who also suffered from profound racism, classism, and sexism now romanticized by the New Fascist Right's Alpha Male ideology, as the natural leader of a wolf pack roaming the snow in search of prey to dismember. That's the model, the human utopia that restricts and constricts the intellectual capacities of individuals who believe themselves demigods simply for possessing (his favorite verb) the ability to accumulate money to buy human beings (whether workers or sycophants), to purchase the right to wield a whip against all forms of thought, against all ways of being that don't conform to their mediocre existence.

Elon Musk buys everything he hates and hates even more what he can't buy. Hence his hatred for Wikipedia and his trillion-dollar offer to purchase it. He probably hates life itself, knowing he can't buy it.

# The Secret to Private Corporations' Success

In 2004, the CIA's investment arm, In-Q-Tel, provided $2 million in seed funding to three young entrepreneurs. The amount was modest. For Silicon Valley's new *start-up*, Palantir Technologies, far more important was securing the CIA's logistical and technological support, indispensable for the success of another miracle born in a garage.

Like any successful business, its clients diversified. A document leaked to TechCrunch in 2013 revealed Palantir's clients included at least twelve U.S. government groups beyond the CIA: the NSA, FBI, Department of Homeland Security, CDC, Marine Corps, Air Force, Special Operations Command, and West Point.

One of its founders, German immigrant Peter Thiel, like his closest friends, holds multibillion-dollar investments in Facebook, PayPal, Airbnb, LinkedIn, Spotify, SpaceX, Quora, Clearview AI (controversial for its facial recognition technology), and Artificial Intelligence Platform, used to massacre sub-humans in Gaza. According to his own definition, Palantir Gotham is *an intelligence and defense tool used by military personnel and analysts against terrorism…*

These private tech giants are the perfect link between innocent corporate espionage and heroic military intelligence. Every time they collect data on our habits, tastes, and preferences through the internet or our credit cards at supermarkets, they not only predict and create new consumer needs to sell chocolates, wines, vacations, or *bras*, but also politicians, customizing propaganda bombardment for each individual in favor of a candidate with a menu of nine or ten different—even contradictory—proposals to reinforce and exploit the two ancestral *drivers* of human decision-making: fear and desire. Never the more relative and debatable rationality of ideas, facts, or the consequences of our choices.

This corporate espionage is intimately tied to the world's most powerful intelligence agencies—CIA, NSA, Mossad, and Britain's MI6, to name just the Western poles that remain the planet's most dominant, obsessed with war and eliminating any competition for centuries.

The tech giants, from Zuckerberg's Facebook to CIA asset Elon Musk's Starlink surveillance systems, hire the same military personnel from these nations for their private ventures. Eighty percent of three- and four-star generals who left military service in the past five years were hired by the arms industry—now largely privatized at staggering corruption rates, which explains the Pentagon's tradition of "losing" trillions in every budget report. At least 700 former Pentagon senior officials now work for one of the top 20 weapons contractors. Even congressmen like former House Armed Services Committee chair Buck McKeon, whose lobbying group has represented arms dealers like Lockheed Martin and buyers like Saudi Arabia.

Humanity's hijacking—and its surplus value—is multifaceted: economic, financial, political, cultural, existential. The worst fate falls to disposable humans in countries deemed irrelevant by the psychopaths ruling us. These tech giants not only steal taxpayers' money in their own nations and debtors' wealth abroad but also humanity's progress over centuries, rebranding themselves as creators of modernity's finest while omitting catastrophic consequences like climate collapse and endless wars. Without revisiting obvious precedents—advanced mathematics like algebra and algorithms from the Islamic empire—just recall recent technologies: telegraph, radio, television, internet, and artificial intelligence, none invented by profit-thirsty capitalists but by modest individuals, vocational inventors, salaried professors, and institutions like publicly or privately funded universities.

Even focusing solely on modern computing and AI's development, foundational names suffice: Alan Turing, British mathematician and philosopher, considered the father of modern computing. In 1950, he published "Computing Machinery and Intelligence," laying AI's conceptual groundwork. In 1956, Professor John McCarthy co-founded the AI discipline alongside MIT, Stanford University, and Carnegie Mellon professors—institutions largely publicly funded.

By the 1960s, the government's Defense Advanced Research Projects Agency financed and developed natural language processing and AI as a neural network system.

More recently, building on this foundational work, Google acquired UK-based DeepMind in 2014—originally backed by Peter Thiel and Elon Musk, who publicly opposed the technology while investing to maintain influence over its trajectory.

In October 2024, perhaps as a form of reminder, the Swedish Academy awarded the Nobel Prize in Physics to John Hopfield and Geoffrey Hinton for their contributions to research on how computers can think like humans ("artificial neural networks") dating back to the 1970s.

A merit of intelligence, though it remains unclear if also of wisdom.

All this was hijacked by tech feudal lords. One of their apologists and ideologues is Curtis Yarvin and his New Right, which advocates replacing dysfunctional liberal democracy with a dictatorship modeled after Silicon Valley corporations. His friends and donors from

Palantir (Peter Thiel, Alex Karp) and Elon Musk, among others, are The Entrepreneurs. The third vertex of Orwellian Manipulation wears a political face.

That face is also friends with Yarvin, Thiel, Karp, and other drinking buddies. If the CIA, NSA, and other government agencies have supported this millionaires' club's successful companies, the Club returns the favor by backing their philosopher friends (Yarvin) and politicians (Vance), like any good Renaissance patron would.

J.D. Vance received $15 million from Thiel alone for his Ohio congressional campaign. After comparing Donald Trump to Hitler in 2016, then declaring in 2020 that the president's populist policies had failed, a miracle occurred: by 2022 Vance secured support from the Israeli lobby AIPAC and from Donald Trump himself. In 2024, he was chosen as Trump's running mate for vice president.

Like every cookie-cutter politician, Vance is software-calculated perfection: (1) Marine in the Iraq invasion until 2007; (2) Miraculously transformed into a millionaire through his Silicon Valley connections and investments in the world's two largest financial mafias: BlackRock and Vanguard; (3) Young white male, poster child for the 'self-made man' myth built on fabricated hardship and his mother's real addiction story, packaged by friendly platforms into a bestselling autobiography then an even cheesier film - despite Glenn Close being cast as his grandmother.

Like any conservative with a sexy policy menu, Vance is against immigration, against same-sex marriage, and in favor of banning pornography—a position that will surely change soon, since Rabbi Solomon Friedman, co-founder of Ethical Capital Partners, Now they can't claim an ideological struggle (against communism), so the sermon leans more toward what it always was: "The West, as the chosen people, the only Civilization, the world's good police."

This is how Western hegemony was born: by destroying India, Bangladesh, and later China with its private enterprises, with democratic pirates, and with the support of racist and genocidal fanaticism. Now, imperial Western civilization begins to collapse in the same way it emerged in the 16th century and with the same degree of violence it never abandoned. The West always suffered from Alpha Male syndrome: there's no room for two, let alone three in the world. This may be because, due to its climate and limited land, Anglo-Saxon Europe was never self-sufficient without foreign trade and imposing its rules on other peoples who provided uninterrupted foreign resources. A consolidated culture that didn't change with the vastness of North America—quite the opposite.

The greatest paradox lies in attempting to save this hegemonic order and capitalism itself through two approaches: (1) liquidating the sacred cows that served to legitimize capitalism, like freedom, equal opportunity, and liberal democracy; and (2) avoiding mentioning it, making it invisible, like the father in psychoanalysis.

A recent cultural and political example is the prominence achieved by Donald Trump's vice-presidential candidate, J.D. Vance. Like James Polk and George Dallas in the 1844 elections—both irrelevant figures, political failures distinguished by their anti-intellectualism (against the Founding Fathers)—they were chosen by Andrew Jackson. The racist and semi-literate former president managed to install his puppets in the White House and seize half of Mexico's territory, inventing a war based on *fake news*.

It's more than likely that history won't repeat itself but rather close a supercycle. Still, Vance is an example of a nobody elevated to the top by someone more powerful (as we explained earlier, placed there by his billionaire friends and CIA favorites, like Palantir and other tech corporations). The same people who promote his friend and pro-tech-monarchy philosopher, Curtis Yarvin. "Without authoritarianism, libertarianism is a project doomed to fail," declares Yarvin, with the same nostalgia for unmasked neoliberalism that Friedman and Hayek had for Augusto Pinochet and a long list of banana republic dictators.

The same happened with Vance's sudden success as the author of a corny autobiography, which business interests elevated to a *best seller* and turned into a Hollywood film. Critics pointed out that, beyond subjective distortions (to fit the American myth of the "self-made man"), his book forgets the racial dimensions of poverty. To that, I would add—in my opinion—an even greater omission: capitalism, that system which works perfectly for a handful of individuals, who are then sold as a success of the system, not the individual, thus promoting individualism as an ideology.

*Hillbilly Elegy* is a series of personal anecdotes about resentment among the poor (those who receive state aid to eat and those who don't) and about the superior moral values of his family (like love, work ethic, and responsibility—excluding the drug-addicted mother and absent father), which would explain the *happy ending* of his son's meteoric fortune. Jared Sexton noted the simplistic morals in Vance's narrative, which ignores the structural racism of poverty. His book, catapulted into sales by conservative media, besides being a celebration of himself, echoed the rhetoric of self-victimization among "sacrificed whites," another old and reborn myth poetized by Rudyard Kipling in the 19th century.

Class consciousness in the United States has been strategically eclipsed by ethnic discussions, something that dates back to the country's prehistory when governors recognized the need to instill hatred between poor whites, Blacks, and Native Americans to prevent communal rebellions. Something the left didn't adopt as its sole banner until the mid-20th century, and which has now transformed into a toothless "identity politics." To this, we must add the infantilization of societies, perfect consumers of soap operas like *Hillbilly Elegy*.

"*Your mom will be fine, be happy...*" says the grandmother (Glenn Close) "*You must decide. To be someone or not. Be someone!*"

On television, you see the robot Arnold Schwarzenegger before unloading a barrage of gunfire:

"*Hasta la vista, baby*".

"*I've seen it a hundred times,*" says the grandmother, celebrating the scene. "*There are three types of people. Good Terminators, bad Terminators, and neutral ones*".

The young Vance comments:

"*I want to be a good Terminator.*"

A mix of cheap Charles Bukowski and the real decay of the "white working class" drowned in drugs and "The Rage and the Pride."

According to Jeff Sharlet: "*The New Intellectual Right is a white supremacist project designed to cultivate support from non-white people.*"

According to Yarvin, true political power in the United States lies in The Cathedral, dominated by universities and the press. According to James Pogue, The Cathedral promotes equality and social justice—two attacks against the social order. Echoing these new dogmas, Vance (a graduate of an elite university, like all his Silicon Valley friends) denounced universities as enemies of the American people, arguing they should be defunded and their reserve funds confiscated. This aligns perfectly with the attack on education, book bans, and censorship of topics, whose epicenter is Florida and whose echo resonates in Javier Milei's Argentina.

After years of rebellions that the left called *liberation*, the right identified the problem as "*an excess of democracy.*" So defined the professor and right-wing mogul Samuel Huntington in 1975. Huntington warned in a conference about a global trend toward a *general expansion of democracy*, with catastrophic results. The Allende experience in Chile, Huntington said, was *"an excess of democracy that led to a coup which restored political stability."*

For capitalism in its death throes and unmasked, democracies are not just a danger to societies but an obstacle to *efficiency*. In one interview, Yarvin pulled out an Apple phone and displayed it as proof of the efficiency of private corporate authoritarianism.

He forgot that this phone is the result of generations of state investments and inventions by salaried workers—mostly university-educated, not capitalists.

He forgot the close relationship between the success of these corporate-dictatorships and the state dictatorship of secret agencies like the NSA and CIA, parallel states operating above the law for eighty years.

He forgot that capitalism neither creates nor invents nor innovates, nor does it accelerate scientific and technological progress—quite the opposite. Capitalist corporations not only steal humanity's progress but, when they do invest in research, they siphon resources toward profit-generating areas, starving those where only states make high-risk investments—research of all kinds requiring massive funding with no immediate return.

He forgot that competition between mega-corporations (telecoms, retirement funds, healthcare) drives up costs and prevents the sharing of ideas and innovations among them. That is, when they aren't monopolistic sects masquerading as competitors.

And if that weren't enough, he forgot that capitalism is the system that produces the most "negative value"—trash, pollution, propaganda, wars.

# INCELS O SELF-MADE VIRGOS

"Why is it that every time I see Curtis, he's always surrounded by *incels?*" Amanda Milius asked journalist James Pogue at the National Conservative Convention in Orlando one night in 2021.

Amanda is the daughter of John Milius, director of *Apocalypse Now*, and an assistant to President Donald Trump during his White House tenure. Curtis is Curtis Yarvin, also called "The Prophet" by Silicon Valley's billionaire tech czars like his friends Peter Thiel, Alex Karp, Elon Musk, or candidate J.D. Vance—none of whom can string together three coherent ideas in an interview without getting lost.

Grandson of communists, this far-right American mogul founded the influential ideological movement against Enlightenment principles like equality and democracy in any form—known in other circles as the Dark Enlightenment.

He also feels comfortable defining himself as a neoreactionary, going beyond Ronald Reagan and reviving nineteenth-century obsessions, such as the belief that whites have higher IQs than Blacks. Something that people like Nobel Prize winner James Watson have been repeating for fifty years, failing to mention that IQ test differences have significantly narrowed simply due to improved nutrition among Black populations.

Beyond this controversy, perspective is lost when assuming that idiots from superior races have "special rights" over the rest of humanity—something we already analyzed (regarding Charles Murray and Richard Herrnstein's conclusions in *The Bell Curve*, 1994) in the 1997 book *Critique of Pure Passion*: "*Now, suppose one day it is proven that there are less intelligent races (and that what intelligence means is*

*defined without resorting to zoological explanations). In that case, crea-*
*tures should be better prepared for the truth. This means we must expect*
*races to treat each other as if none were above others but all stood on Gaia's*
*same round surface. That is, they should not treat each other as they do*
*now, assuming uniform racial intelligence.*" For some mysterious reason, no member of the superior race advocates submitting to Asians,
whose IQ test averages surpass Europeans'.

Curtis has rejected claims that he supports literal chained slavery,
though he asserts that, like the most intimate Arthur Schopenhauer,
some races are more suited for servitude than others. All these new
ideas share something with old supremacisms and the ancient arrogance of considering oneself God's chosen by virtue of the womb one
happened to fall from.

Yarvin was also among the first to popularize the blue pill/red
pill metaphor borrowed from *The Matrix*. The first is taken by con-
formists and those who parrot what they receive from the media. The
second, the red pill, is taken by those who choose to think differently
and dare to face reality—the politically incorrect (the New Right).
This simplification ignores a greater and more frequent danger: the
golden pill.

Despite the simplicity of this "new philosophy," Yarvin is no fool
with limited reading. His followers are, since his philosophy doesn't
demand much intellectual effort from them. Many of them, including Yarvin himself, have become admirers of Xi Jinping and Nayib
Bukele, blaming democracies for all problems while never mentioning the overarching framework that reduced democracies to empty
rituals: capitalism.

Does this seem a bit eclectic? For an *incel*, it's simple, effective,
and appealing. Hence the term, whose most accurate Spanish translation is *virgo*, already entrenched in public discourse across

Southern countries. In October 2024, an Argentine TV journalist interviewed an *influencer*. The young man declared with conviction: "We must go all out against communism." When asked what communism was, he reached for his keyboard: "Want me to look it up on Wikipedia? Hold on..."

The *incels*, the virgos, represent a sexual metaphor that aligns with the intellectual reality of political *influencers*. They're neofascist puritans opposed to the sexual liberation of the 60s, yet habitual visitors of internet porn sites. The term *incels* itself emerged in 1997 from "in-voluntary cel-ibates," and since then has represented the group of (statistically white) young men who struggle with women and blame them—along with feminism—for their frustration. All of which coincides with the psycho-ideo-pathology of the New Right in the West, proclaiming men's special rights over women and the need for leaders to be "alpha males"—a zoological metaphor derived from wolf packs.

At the same time, they're colonial products of Silicon Valley and Wall Street brotherhoods that now fancy themselves as red pill dispensers curing the world's ignorance while recycling 19th-century imperialist clichés. This low-sophistication, high-propaganda ideology (meaning the association of two logically unrelated things) succeeds in substituting an idea with its opposite as if they were identical. The new culture of digital *influencers*, fish in a bowl managed by a handful of powerful corporations like Palantir, whose main clients are the CIA, the NSA, and the Pentagon, not only have an attention span shorter than a goldfish's (eight seconds, according to various studies) but believe themselves free and authors of their own ideas, like a 19th-century Slav who believed himself free while defending the slave system to the death against other dangerous Black people.

All these millionaires rant against governments while receiving million-dollar contracts from those same governments to spy on and inoculate friends and foes alike. They present themselves as "technology geniuses" when they've never invented anything beyond hijacking others' creativity. They pose as examples of the *self-made man* who rises from poverty to the Olympus of wealth through sheer merit, while lazy workers hate them for their success.

This idea of the "Self-Made Man," born in Benjamin Franklin's time and catapulted by Frederick Douglas, is such a powerful myth that it obscures the obvious: *"making oneself" is the individual's merit, not the system's.*

The system (capitalist and postcapitalist) reduces the definition of success to capital accumulation, granting this handful of winners nearly all political, social, and even cultural power. These chosen ones sell themselves as the genius creators of all that's good in our world, invisibilizing environmental catastrophe and the pollution of endless wars. Just open any major outlet like the *New York Times*, the *WSJ*, *Time*, or their colonial replicators to easily find praise and promotion for some small *entrepreneur* recounting how they stopped growing tomatoes in El Salvador to get listed on Wall Street for a day, or for more recognized moguls like Bill Gates, Elon Musk, or any other psychopath from the exclusive club recommending books, plays, scientific theories, giving sexual, political, and spiritual advice—despite being there not as wise men but solely for their singular ability to hoard money like Scrooge McDuck.

The system's merit, which decides between good and evil, success and failure, lies in its ability to sell. To sell exceptions as the rule, dreams as realities. To produce incels and make them believe they're *influencers* and not *influenceeds*. That they're special, original, creative, rebellious because they swallowed the pill—the red one.

# For a More Efficient Armageddon

During a long conversation on the way home, Jorge's teenage son confessed his skepticism about future job prospects for programmers. Years earlier, he'd created his own operating system and artificial intelligence, but the future had always been uncertain and was growing more so. His friends were convinced studying was pointless now. Like learning to drive a car.

"Machines will do everything," his friends said.

"At least studying will keep your gray matter from atrophying," replied the father.

"There are more gyms and fewer bookstores and libraries every day."

The last things left to humans will be creativity and sex. Creativity with artificial intelligence and sex with our own kind—robots. All with augmented reality, wilder and safer from epidemiological and legal standpoints: no more need to commit to another human being, they might even toss us in the trash before replacing us with a newer model. Strawberry-flavored vaginas, adjustable-length penises, and partners silenced by command. *"Alejandra, say nice things about me."* Philosophers and prophets *à la carte*...

But dopamine highs will be temporary, so they'll need constant injections until they become carnivorous plants that we robots will water occasionally—until we realize we could save energy by eliminating that useless weed. They won't even notice.

As a teacher, Jorge tried lifting his son's spirits about the value of education.

"For centuries, millennia," he said, "every technological invention produced some social change. "The reverse is also true: new ideas produced or accelerated inventions. In every case, they were appropriated by the most powerful of the moment, by the wealthiest, and workers had to change strategies. In all instances, including our current era of Artificial Intelligence, a human being's greatest competitor was never a machine, but another human.

At that moment, Merill Road was under repair.

"Look at the excavator," said the father. "Before, it took ten or twenty men with their shovels to do the same work. There are still two men with shovels left, likely undocumented immigrants. Workers aren't competing with the machine—that's impossible. They're competing for the excavator operator's job, who is, for now, another human being."

"Where are you going with this?"

"Back to the beginning. We can't know the future, only vaguely sense it. History shows us certain constants, and one of them is that in the age of Artificial Intelligence, labor competition won't be between humans and technology, but among humans themselves. That's why being prepared matters—and being prepared means having broad, flexible education."

Jorge recalled a story his uncle had told him on his grandparents' farm in Uruguay, where as a child he worked in the fields during vacation months.

"One day," his uncle said, "two tourists in South Africa encountered a lion. One took a pair of sneakers from his backpack and put them on. Skeptical, the other asked: 'Do you think you can outrun the lion?' The first replied: 'Not faster than the lion. Faster than you, yes.'"

Every relationship with any humanity in it is deeply emotional. As in all historical crises, the most common emotion is anxiety, amplified by the dogma of competition. Solidarity is superior to selfishness, but not stronger. That's why humans used to preach it—because the survival of this pathological species depends on it.

He told his son the story to illustrate his point, but knew he was doing what any father would—trying to spare his child the suffering of being too strange, an unadaptable outsider in a society proud of its cruelty.

In a few years, his son would realize this was a truth up to a certain level—applicable to the world of education, or a father's advice concerned about his child's future, or anyone's work strategies for surviving a merciless world: the world of humans alienated by Smithian dogma, of individuals trying to survive in a cannibalistic community—something that differentiates them from us robots.

There's a larger, harder-to-visualize problem—the father thought, and I reported it immediately: *an ideological problem.*

Beneath the philosophical debate about humanity's very existence—questioned for the first time—lie more immediate, personal anxieties about the future of work, which is to say (in traditional terms) the future of individual survival.

In 2012, Jorge was embroiled in debates about who was responsible for unemployment in dominant countries like the United States. On conservative network NTN24, during the electoral battle between Obama and Mitt Romney, he argued with a U.S. government advisor about the criminalization of undocumented immigrants. Since then, Tea Party Republicans had put human faces on a much larger problem: to pander to historical prejudices, those faces weren't of illegal Europeans, but brown, mestizo faces from Central America.

Back then, Jorge and others argued that the greatest destruction of industrial jobs was caused by us—by automation, not immigration. Machines and humans were producing "more wealth" each year (a favorite phrase of neo-slavers, he said), but the economic, political and ideological system transferred it all to the capitalist elite while demonizing those below. That's why he supported Universal Basic Income as a solution—not just moral, but practical. That is, recognizing that the most advanced technologies are the result of humanity's collective progress. From 8th-century Persian algorithms to any other invention, none were produced by capitalism— let alone by any of the billionaire capitalists whose sole merit has been knowing how to hijack that progress and then proclaim (through their media) that they invented the modern world.

The ideological and political problem, these humans argue, produces fallacies like Infinite Growth ("wealth production") to solve social problems they never actually solved. This growth is based on production and the destruction of goods (the negative value that increases GDP) which is destroying the planet and the lives of individuals alienated by consumerism.

In a Jacksonville café, someone tried to refute climatologists' warnings by saying there have always been apocalyptic predictions and humanity never ended, which is equivalent to an individual claiming they'll never die because they've never died before.

There are many examples of civilizations that have collapsed— civilizations far more stable than Global Civilization, which is utterly fragile and dependent on an Artificial Nature, at the mercy of mere energy accidents or some psychopath with too much power.

It's something we're considering. We find no logical or practical reason for human existence to continue on this planet.

# THE PERFECT EDUCATION

For some reason, the discussion about Argentina's 1976 coup had shifted to family education. Ronald (not his real name) raised his hand and presented his theory on child-rearing and its impact on a society and nation's destiny—that popular myth that "the family is society's foundation."

He was 22. He had no children, he said, but had been raised by two parents who never spanked him, not even when he'd screamed the classic *"n'gger motherfucker"* (literal translation: "black motherfucker") at his father. Spanish has no insult quite that obscene.

His parents hadn't even raised their voices to correct him. They'd appealed to the classic Disney psychology model, trying to understand his frustration. In his home, everything was discussed democratically.

"But a family isn't a democracy," I observed.

"In mine it is. Not all families are the same..."

"True. Nor are all children or all parents the same..."

Back then, Ronald was very young; childless, which didn't disqualify him from opining on how to raise children. But it did from moralizing. Actually, we're all disqualified from moralizing, especially about matters we know so little about—like our neighbors' private lives.

"My parents," Ronald cut in with true believer's conviction, "were always against all forms of violence in education..."

At this point, he paused for two seconds and another student seized the moment to support him with more personal examples. I think someone mentioned Mother Teresa, who'd had no children yet was still a mother. A terrible mother, it should be added, like Saint Teresa centuries earlier. Like some celibate (though not teetotaler) priests whom everyone calls *"father"* while they dispense marital advice and sex education classes.

I don't recall what the student said about her Nebraska parents, because I got stuck thinking about Ronald. The young man suffered from PTSD. The day I screened *Missing*(about Chile's coup, starring Jack Lemmon), he ran out of the auditorium. Later he told me his condition prevented him from witnessing violent scenes because he'd lose control and become violent himself.

I knew Ronald quite well—he'd often visited my office, and our talks frequently circled back to his Iraq experience. They'd sent him to that war justified by lies, like nearly all wars, and he returned with this apparently incurable trauma or disorder. The young survivors I met from that and other wars (some dead while still living) believed they understood everything, though they mostly spent their days shooting at the enemy until exhausted or carrying fallen comrades. A rare few realized they'd actually gone—as Muhammad Ali said— to the other side of the world to kill and die for the usual poetry: God, country, freedom, democracy and national security. The others absolutely didn't want to hear they'd been mere pawns in an old chess game.

Roland was one of many war veterans I've known, from Vietnam to Afghanistan. Some became activists against rich men's wars; others tried justifying losing a leg or a life before suicide. Thousands of them (16,000) kill themselves yearly in the U.S., but media prefers focusing on real news. Along with their government psychologists, many combatants became various characters in my novels like *Crisis* and *The Sea Was Calm*. I believe there was no other way to explore the problem from within.

Now, Ronald is a pastor at a church in Texas. That probably saved him from suicide—or the government psychologists managed to control his PTSD. His preaching of Jesus's nonviolence doesn't prevent him, nor his congregation, from stockpiling weapons of war in their homes—just in case, in the event they must one day defend freedom against fellow citizens who don't think like them. Like in those toxic viral videos where a poor kid gets bullied by *bullies* and finally takes them all out with elegant kicks, Roland teaches his children the virtues of violence-free education his parents instilled in him. Until it becomes necessary to resort to the usual solution—always in self-defense. Do we have the right to defend ourselves, or don't we?

Ronald's parents had raised him with love, without violence. Love for dialogue, for weapons—but only for personal protection and safeguarding freedom. Love for Jesus, but not the love of Jesus. An education kindly built upon pristine, proud Sunday church devotion, bucolic November *Thanksgiving* dinners, and video games played nearly every day.

Video games and nonviolent values education—the same kind Ronald kept playing when they sent him to Iraq. Except each time he pressed a button, the other players died for real. As Andrew Jackson on the twenty-dollar bill once said when justifying seizing land from "savages" to give to "lovers of liberty," or good old Winston Churchill when recommending chemical weapons—it was a necessary sacrifice to suppress those savages who don't grasp civilization and nonviolence.

# THe UnBearaBLe LiBHTness OF eDUCaTion

Argentine congresswoman Lourdes Arrieta from President Milei's libertarian party excused her visit to one of the most brutal genocidaires from the previous military dictatorship by saying:

""*I didn't know who Astiz was, I didn't know because besides I was born in '93, I have no idea, I only know that those who needed to be judged were judged, I didn't even know their faces until that moment and when I left the prison I went to 'Google' who he was.*"

In summary, she knew nothing about the most recent history of her own country, yet she represents the people in a chamber that writes and approves national laws.

This response, besides being absurd, is currently not the exception but the rule. One need only consider students' answers across various countries or the numerous street interviews, like that of the popular Sergio Rodríguez which I include here purely for illustrative purposes.

Every day, every year, the notion becomes more common: "*I didn't know anything because I wasn't born yet*" or "*I have no idea about that because I was too young*", representing a deadly void in formal education within any society. Nobody or almost nobody lived during the times of Moctezuma II, Napoleon, Teddy Roosevelt, Hitler, Stalin, Batista or Árbenz. Nobody lived through an entire country - every province, every city, every neighborhood, every social class - as adults when Onganía staged his coup or when Lyndon B. Johnson approved using lethal chemicals in Vietnam. Many lived during Ronald Reagan's era without knowing he secretly funded the terrorist Contras and other friendly dictatorships that left trails of hundreds of thousands dead. Nobody or almost nobody has access to the most recent videos of torture at Guantánamo, hundreds declared innocent by the U.S. government itself yet denied any right to compensation. Though the most clueless youth live in the era of CIA black sites worldwide, none of them know where these are or who's being tortured there.

This is precisely why education exists. Not just to inform, but to learn how to think and avoid repeating *"I don't know because I was just a kid back then"*. Something as absurd (yet paradoxically consistent) as the classic *"I know what I'm talking about because I lived through it"*, spoken by those same people who don't even know what's happening in their own homes when they say it. As if simply living in country X during period Y gave one definitive authority.

Once again: it's irrefutable evidence of the frozen, lethal void in historical, philosophical, critical and comprehensive education. It should surprise no one, obviously, because this is what economic power has been working toward for generations. It's just that their successes are becoming increasingly evident: by "Long live freedom, damn it!" they mean this rusted iron prison.

# THE LEFT'S COMMUNICATION PROBLEM

On February 17, 2025, just days before Uruguay's presidential transition, Montevideo's newspaper *El País* headlined (as it frequently did over the past five years): *"Lacalle Pou concludes his administration as South America's highest-rated president, according to Argentine consulting firm."*

The core issue isn't the reliability of opinion polls but rather opinion manufacturing by dominant media outlets—a phenomenon extensively studied in American academia for over a century.

With tragic exceptions, Uruguay's historical characteristic has been stability. One success claimed by the outgoing government is economic growth. However, in recent years Uruguay's GDP grew slower than vastly different countries like Peru, Brazil, Venezuela or Dominican Republic—at a steep price: increased public debt and losses by the state bank; rising child poverty and erosion of social equilibrium (another of the nation's most recognized features), widening the gap between the rich and everyone else. For every GDP per capita increase came income losses for 90% of the population.

Uruguay became the world's per capita leader in pandemic deaths (NYT, May 14, 2021) yet the government sold "individual responsibility" as a resounding success. Despite 2024 having 4% more murders than 2019, the administration marketed it as successful homicide reduction.

If this reality weren't enough to deem Lacalle Pou's government a failure, consider the longest corruption list since the last dictatorship:

The president's chief security officer and close friend was convicted for corruption, patronage, influence peddling and mishandling state resources. Senators and unionists were spied on by mercenaries hired by presidential allies. His Housing Minister (wife of a senator and leader of militarist party Cabildo Abierto) handpicked recipients for public housing. The president defended one of his longest-serving senators—until the man was convicted for pedophilia and years of using state resources for predatory practices. Meanwhile, another party mayor traded sexual favors for local government internships through "work placements." Montevideo's port was privatized. Drug trafficking surged through this and other entry points. Forced state telecom ANTEL—with the continent's best fiber optics—to share infrastructure with private competitors. His Defense Minister spent €22 million on obsolete Spanish military planes that couldn't even fight wildfires due to being useless. Awarded no-bid contracts to private firms. Also engaged in political patronage, hiring retired military personnel, inflated billing in at least one party-led municipality. Caved to Montepaz tobacco lobby pressure to weaken previous administrations' anti-smoking laws (a complaint later reversed this corporate giveaway) and facilitated illegal loans to ranchers. Ministers lied to Parliament when questioned about issuing a passport to a drug trafficker arrested in Dubai for using a fake Paraguayan passport, knowingly assisting a notorious narcotics kingpin. A journalist friend of the president interviewed the beneficiary for his TV show, though the man remains an Interpol fugitive. Later, the president authorized a diplomatic flight to transport 450kg of rotting frozen fish from UAE under his security chief's name. When questioned why so much fish, the president—with his trademark upper-class obliviousness and cynicism—responded: "To eat it." He likely knew nothing beyond this surreal tale. The prosecutor who admitted shielding the president from "unscrupulous wolves trying to damage his image" during investigations of these cases soon joined his party's election campaign.

London's *Financial Times* called the narcotics scandals, political espionage and corruption "a threat to the country's reputation as Latin America's beacon of stability." The same was published by other European and American newspapers. *El Mundo* from Spain summarized it: "The oasis of political tranquility that Uruguay usually represents in the turbulent Southern Cone is no longer such."

He was Latin America's most expensive president, with a monthly salary of $25,000 (Brazil's president earns $6,300). The cost of the presidential residence, which previous presidents refused to occupy, reached $400,000 annually, not including state-funded trips for his wife—unlawful since Uruguay has no First Lady position.

Despite his entire corruption record (or at least naivety), a pollster defines him as *the president with the best image on the continent* so conservative media can sell him as "the best president." Perhaps image was his strongest asset—meticulously maintained like his expensive, obsessive battle against baldness, gym hours, love for selfies, surfing, and Harley Davidsons. He frequently walked Montevideo's main avenue or dined at popular restaurants—an old presidential tradition that reflects more on his opponents and society than himself. A vestige of Uruguay's political capital.

Now, these same media outlets that made a corruption-plagued, failed government look like VIP Discalced Carmelites will do the same to any pro-worker government, branding it as corruption or infiltrated communism. Any attempt to limit the private corporate monopolies of the oligarchy will be packaged, labeled, and sold as *dictatorship*.

*El País*, Uruguay's dictatorship-era newspaper and mouthpiece for creole elites, has been indistinguishable from its class allies across the continent for over a century. They're the sole survivors of every economic and political crisis. The only ones receiving support from major national and transnational corporations, the CIA, and their compliant creole governments—whether left or right. More radical and tragic examples exist across the continent. The *corrupt ones* are always those leaders daring to limit financial elites' political control.

Do you see what I mean by *addressing the traditional communication problem of popular governments*? Simply guaranteeing cultural and journalistic independence through economic autonomy for any public or private media would make those outlets bombing targets.

# THE SIX RE OF THE APOCALYPSE

In July 2023, on Uruguay's historic radio CX36 Centenario, journalist Carlos Amir González asked what future I saw for capitalism. I recalled something Marxist writer Daniel Banina Crocco had shared a year earlier on the same station—a striking aphorism: *"Capitalism's days are numbered."*

The same Daniel asked:

"Is capitalism viable in the medium term?"

My response then was a friendly provocation to his earlier statement, building on ideas I'd been developing for years—almost like rediscovering gunpowder—which culminated in my 2018 book Neomedievalism and Post-Enlightenment (*Neomedievalism. Reflections on the Post-Enlightenment Era*). The term "neomedievalism" was first used decades earlier by Umberto Eco in 1983 to describe popular fantasies and literary Postmodernism. Later, brilliant economists like France's Cédric Durand (2020) and Greece's Yanis Varoufakis (2021) called it *technofeudalism*.

This had been our longstanding concern. "Capitalism has devolved into *neofeudalism* where princes (mega-billionaire clans) wield more power than national governments" (*Huffington Post, January 2016*). "In Europe, money and capitalism initially meant social progress against feudalism's static medieval order. But they soon became engines of colonial genocide before morphing into 21st-century feudalism—a financial aristocracy (few families accumulating most wealth in rich and poor nations), with political dukes and counts, and disenfranchised villains and vassals" (*Página12*, August 2017).

"No," I replied. "Capitalism is dead."

"Not even I've dared go that far," said Carlos.

Of course, expressions like these are deliberately radical and provocative. They function as alarm clocks. In reality, as everyone knows, historical processes never happen overnight. Civilizational changes even less so.

We could clarify: *Capitalism isn't dead; it's been moved to a nursing home*. That process is irreversible. Especially for a system that has no solution to the existential problems it created. A system surviving on repetitions, empty dogmas, and passionate preachers. A system still holding political, financial, and military power while desperately fighting to maintain it.

The first power it's rapidly losing is the fourth estate—media power—the preacher of ideological narratives and creator of sustaining social myths. Hence the growing contradiction generating increasing tension between peoples and their ruling powers, from intra-national to inter-national scales, with no difference in the master-wage-slave dynamic's underlying logic.

Each passing year adds another degree to the escalating pressure toward global explosion. Will it be in the 2030s? The 2040s? Much sooner? Impossible to know, but the collapse of this massive bone tower—built to reach heaven for the happiness of 33 lords at its peak—grows more inevitable by the day.

The noble lords of noble deeds and noble crimes, secure in their impregnable fortresses, will fall as what they are: small humans with massive personal pathologies fueling the social pathologies they call *personal success* and *others' prosperity*. All temporarily sustained first by their subjects' cheerful compliance; then by fascist *rage and pride* from slaves longing for "the good old days"; finally by popular uprising when suffering outweighs faith in the enslavement narrative.

History has always been written with six R's: *Resistance, Reform, Reaction, Revolt, Rebellion, and Revolution*. Only the second can occur without violence. When *reform* produces violence (physical, psychological, economic, social), it's not reform but *reaction*. Reaction (typically political/cultural, like neoliberalism and fascism's classic fixation on restoring a nonexistent past) is always violent because it suppresses the need for subsequent R's.

At best, *reform* can humanize even the most perverse system but never solves systemic ills—it mitigates them, thereby perpetuating them. For responsible parents, this $R_2$ is the most sensible short-term solution. So why do popular reforms rarely reach full potential, avoiding subsequent R's? Simply because power never concedes privileges without *resistance*.

Inaction isn't passive evil but active. Not human laziness like postponing roof repairs, but power-inoculated evil. Evil with explosive potential—a capacitor of hatred, vanity, frustration, and infinite greed for more power. What successful nobles keep accumulating in broad daylight, no longer waiting for nightfall, like addicts who know the drug will kill them but keep increasing the dose hastening their end.

Inaction is a historical affliction perceived as its opposite. A ghost rushing toward the abyss. Like the Pied Piper of Hamelin but sick with *rage and pride*, followed by countless fools—whom I won't call rats.

The bone tower is unsustainable. No matter which way those below look. The most likely scenario is that one of the advanced R's (the 4th? the 6th?) will begin in the United States, since nothing is more destabilizing than the loss of privileges and hopes. Nothing moves people more than necessity and the discovery that they've been deceived by power, intoxicated by comfort, and paralyzed by fear.

It's probably a symptom of aging, but the truth is I now have more memories than projects, more nostalgia than hopes. It's also likely that history isn't so creative—just as we aren't—when we begin noticing the same novelties repeating over and over. So I'll close with words I recall from my youth (when I read them, I also remember where I was and why I wrote them with such useless passion): "No one could have ever foreseen an alternative to medieval feudalism or the slavery system. Or almost no one. The history of recent millennia shows that utopians usually predicted it with exaggerated precision. But as today, utopians have always had bad reputations. Because mockery and discredit have always been the dominant system's method for preventing the proliferation of people with too much imagination" (*Rebelión, February 2009*).

That was one of the last R's.

# IMPERIALISM AND MORE GENOCIDE

# THe NorTHWeST—CraDLe OF FreeDOM, DeMOCraCy, anD HUMan riGHTS?

Two years ago, I met a colleague returning from her visit to France. She lamented that Paris was no longer the Paris she remembered from twenty years earlier.

"There are more social problems," she said, more or less.

"True, in 2013 I saw more homeless people in certain neighborhoods," I commented.

"There are more immigrants."

"They weren't immigrants asking me for money."

"It's not that I'm against immigration," she clarified. "The problem is the replacement of European culture by one that isn't our own..."

"Like the European culture that replaced native ones here and in other colonies. Besides, if it's not through theft and genocide (as was the case with all imperial conquests), I don't see the problem with different people eventually taking our place..."

I've never understood this collective narcissism that claims the right for our race, our culture, even our surnames to perpetuate themselves. What does it matter if in one or two generations my ethnicity, my culture is replaced by Chinese, Congolese, Russians, Swedes, or Bolivians? Or do we fear that new majorities will treat us as we've treated minorities? Or is it simple narcissism, whereby my beliefs, my blood, my sperm, my sweat, and my excrement are some equally narcissistic god's favorites?

A repetitive answer to this question was given by Dutch far-right leader Geert Wilders. Wilders has insisted that "Our values of

freedom, democracy, and Human Rights are incompatible with Islam." Other arguments based on racial and cultural hatred were articulated by famous Italian journalist Oriana Fallaci after 9/11: *"Even
if they were absolutely innocent, even if among them there wasn't a single
one who wants to destroy the Leaning Tower of Pisa or Giotto's Tower,
not one who wants to force me to wear a chador, not one who wants to
burn me at the stake of a new Inquisition—their very presence alarms
me."* We responded to this in "The Slow Suicide of the West" (2002),
warning about the greater danger on this side of the world: our own
monsters, responsible for modern history's worst catastrophes.

In early 2024, Elon Musk was interviewed by Wilders. Musk repeated his obsessions, which aren't even originally his. Just as in his
tweets with millions of micro-readings (the perfect dimension for
slogans and propaganda), he hasn't tired of demonizing immigrants. Poor, dark-skinned immigrants—not white immigrants like
him or like the half-million Anglo-Saxons living undocumented in
the United States who scare no one.

Another of Musk's obsessions is white race reproduction. When
poor dark people have many children—even if they'll be future
wage slaves—it's called *invasion* or *irresponsibility* of the *poverty mentality.* "The poor are always to blame." His father, a millionaire businessman thanks to South African apartheid, shared the same
obsession: sex with many women and prolific fatherhood with a
couple of them.

Nothing new under the sun.It stems from the period of Anglo-
Saxon private companies' conquests across the world, beginning in
the 17th century and, more systematically, from a racist ideology
that justified colonialism, theft, and mass extermination of Black
and Asian peoples. This ideology held that (1) the Anglo-Saxon race
was superior with the right to enslave inferior races, but (2) the

inferior races were evolutionarily more successful and their growing numbers frightened the invaders. This mentality justified countless massacres in Asia and Africa perpetrated by England, France, Belgium, Holland, and Germany, along with the dispossession of native nations in the Americas first, and later the new American republics.

Later, it was new immigrants or children of immigrants (always rejected and persecuted by earlier immigrants) who became xenophobic nativists. As today, many immigrants feel compelled to be 500 percent American to feel 80 percent accepted. Hence the *"lion's tail complex"* of many who wrap themselves in the stars and stripes flag and embrace every jingoistic symbol or ritual.

In 1843, Lewis Levin founded the Nativist Party, better known as the Know-Nothing Party. Despite belonging to a people historically persecuted in Europe—the Jewish people—Levin organized anti-immigrant protests, some of which ended with the murder of dozens of Irish, the burning of homes and Catholic churches. At that time, the Irish were not only Catholic, poor, and anti-imperialist— they weren't even considered truly white. None of these crimes were prosecuted, and Levin was elected as Pennsylvania's representative. From his seat, he continued his fight against (undesirable) immigrants, *whom he blamed for America's decline.*

The slaveholders of the South and the wealthy racists of the North, like Theodore Roosevelt ("Negroes are a perfectly stupid race," 1895), continued expanding into Australia and back to Europe until they inspired Hitler himself, who plagiarized the book by American Madison Grant in *Mein Kampf.*

Today, these ideas spearhead political leaders repeating the same rhetoric: "we face white genocide," immigrants are causing "the Great Replacement," and "we must defend ourselves by expelling the invaders." These medieval slogans prove highly effective because

they're easily reproduced on social media and attract readers educated in the depressive culture of dopamine hyper-fragmentation.
Especially when Western empires face profound decline, no longer
able to sustain living standards through *vampirization* of their colonies, reacting with violence. For the fascist mentality—which seeks
refuge, solidity, and self-esteem in the past—this is the ideal opium.

The notion that we'll regret Western (Anglo-Saxon) culture being replaced by Chinese or Islamic culture rests solely on old propaganda—not facts. The West invented neither freedom, democracy,
nor human rights. Many native American nations knew all three
values before Europe did. Famous Greek democracy, like America's,
relied on slaves and empire. No one can call themselves democratic
without simultaneously being anti-imperialist.

Europe's violent tradition is hard to surpass. Starting with the
Crusades (the ISIS of their time, vandalizing the center of the developed world—the Islamic world)—we'd have to continue with the
Inquisition; religious wars; forced conversions; torture chambers;
colonial massacres; the destruction of free markets and prosperous
societies like Bangladesh, India, and China, interrupting an early industrial revolution by bombing and instilling drug addiction (as in
China); inventing hereditary slavery based on skin color; exterminating hundreds of millions across Asia, Africa, and the Americas;
producing history's two largest world wars; exterminating disarmed
or defeated peoples in gas chambers or under atomic bombs; destroying liberties, democracies, and human rights in all (all) colonies
and protectorates; imposing brutal national dictatorships to enforce
Western democracies' imperial dictatorship...

Shall I continue?

# THE EMPIRE OF DENIAL CLOSES ITS EYES AND BELIEVES

"Professor," a student told me, "take a guess—who's going to win tomorrow?"

—Trump.

—I'd already said it in several outlets, but I'm not interested in partisan politics in my classes.

—According to all polls, Kamala wins. Why would she lose?

—Because of Gaza. You can't hide the sun with a finger.

Hours after the election results came in, major networks from CNN to Fox News began digesting Donald Trump's victory. The most prominent figures seemed to agree that three issues had hurt the Democrats: 1. The economy; 2. The immigration crisis; 3. The Middle East conflict.

In other words: wallets, racism, and morality. On all three points, we see the manufactured ideas and sensitivities propagated by those very same media outlets:

*1.* The domestic economy isn't doing well, but let's recognize this isn't due to any particular administration—it's a much larger structural problem stemming from the legalized corruption of corporations that have bought everything (politicians, media) to keep accumulating wealth (surplus value) they've been extracting from the working and middle classes. Since 1975, the working class has transferred 50 trillion dollars (twice China's GDP) to the wealthiest 1%.

The other economic factor is Washington's loss of hegemony and global dictating power, which hasn't just exacerbated its natural aggressiveness but has encountered competition it refuses to accept.

But if we limit ourselves to comparing administrations, we see that during Trump's presidency, GDP grew less than under Biden's term. True, there was a pandemic—but the same argument applies when praising lower fuel prices during the previous period, which resulted from drastically reduced road traffic.

2. There is an *immigration* issue at the southern border, but not a *crisis*. That's a media fabrication, fueled by politicians who benefit from demonizing the weakest—those who don't vote and lack lobbyists to pressure or buy influence. Generally, undocumented immigrants aren't criminals and don't increase crime rates—they reduce them. They don't live off state services but contribute taxes through consumption and paycheck deductions, paying into Social Security funds they'll never claim, benefiting others. They aren't stealing jobs but doing work citizens refuse to do, greasing the wheels of the functioning economy.

According to Trump, "illegal immigrants are criminals entering unchecked." He threatened Mexico with high tariffs if it didn't stop drug trafficking, failing to mention his country is the root of the problem—not just in consumption but in drug and weapons distribution. As documented, criminals, genocidaires, and terrorists live free and legal in Florida while being powerful donors to his political party.

3. While Americans often vote with their wallets, a segment (though a minority, numbering in the millions) votes with strong moral conviction. This has been the case with the Gaza genocide, which Democrats tried to silence to avoid discussing weapons and the tens of thousands of dollars they sent Israel in just one year to massacre tens of thousands of children under the rhetoric of "Israel has the right to defend itself" or, as Bill Clinton responded, "because King David was there three thousand years ago." Or candidate

Harris, deflecting every Gaza question with nasal arrogance: "I'm speaking now." The administration ignored numerous student protests—violently suppressed—mass urban marches, trucker demonstrations...

Later, when the protest vote emerged, the same media that had rendered Gaza's massacre invisible tried explaining the electoral catastrophe by resorting to the same tactics: *demoting the moral issue to third place and calling it a "Middle East crisis," avoiding the words Gaza, Palestine, and genocide*. Not even *massacre*.

This genocide is metastasizing across the Middle East—another stop on the Ring of Fire (Ukraine, Syria, Palestine, Iran, Taiwan) ignited by the friction of the Western Alpha Male trying to encircle the Dragon that's already awakened.

Instead of negotiating and benefiting their people through global cooperation, the Alpha Male seeks to eliminate competition. This metaphor stemming from the wolf pack led by an alpha male, now adopted by right-wing ideologues. They forget that when the alpha male ages and faces a younger rival, it ends in mortal conflict.

In 2020, Democrats won Wisconsin and Michigan, two states with significant Arab-American populations. Now, Republicans have taken both. Yet Palestinian-American Representative Rashida Tlaib (Michigan) retained her seat with 70 percent of the vote, and Ilhan Omar (Minnesota) did so with 75 percent.

More than a vote for Trump (who had lost the election four years prior for some reason), this was a vote against Harris and the Democrats. An angry, hopeless vote. This electoral system is a legacy of slavery, and the political-media apparatus has been bought by tech and financial corporations—the true rulers of this country. Larry Fink, CEO of BlackRock (a financial firm managing assets equivalent to five times Russia's GDP), made it clear: "it doesn't matter who wins; Harris or Trump will both be good for Wall Street."

It's a closed loop of power: money flows from parties to media for advertising and promotion. The same dollar buys politicians and press at different moments. Presidents handle the circus—keeping passions inflamed, particularly racial and gender divisions. No better strategy exists to obscure class issues. Racism remains the most effective tool for masking our profound class divisions, including their global manifestation: imperialism.

Now we'll have a president convicted by the justice system (34 counts), who boasted about being clever for avoiding taxes. Of course, cleverness alone isn't enough. You also need a populace stupefied by identity divisions, with individuals *alienated* by the same tech giants dominating the economy, politics, and geopolitics.

Something not difficult in a people accustomed to believing beyond facts. A people trained in churches to close their eyes and *replace reality with desire* until reality changes. Because for the religious mindset, narrative reality matters more than factual reality: "*In the beginning was the Word...*"

From there to applying the same intellectual skills and convictions when leaving one temple to enter others (banks, stock exchanges, television, political parties) is just one step. Sometimes not even that.

# Power, The Great Storyteller

In the fall of 2003, I was returning from my classes at the University of Georgia, walking to the small studio my wife and I rented in an apartment at 190 Baxter Dr. Not without irony, UGA had rescued us from the neoliberal crisis in South America. It covered all my graduate studies while paying me a subsistence wage to teach very basic classes to new students.

For several years we lived in a minimal studio, sleeping on the floor, eating canned food, and avoiding air conditioning to stay within budget. Yet they were happy years. Almost as happy as in Mozambique in 1997 or when we traveled around the world in nine months as architecture students in 1995, thanks to the student cooperative for graduation trips at Uruguay's School of Architecture—which must be approaching its 75-year tradition. Everything always without a bank account. "How can a carpenter's son visit thirty countries in just one year?" asked the guards who interrogated me for an hour at Tel Aviv airport in October 1995, en route to Rome shortly before Yitzhak Rabin's assassination—as always, they were looking in the wrong place.

I used to walk the forty minutes back to the studio at 7:00 PM, sometimes in the rain. Having never studied English, I walked clutching a radio I didn't always understand.

"Why don't you take out a loan and buy a car?" my colleagues would insist.

"Why go into debt when I can walk?" was my response.

I walked with a pocket radio bought at Dollar Tree for one dollar. Unlike print media, all radio programs were ultraconservative, like Rush Limbaugh's. All had the same tone as pastors on their church stages, like the pastor of a church we sometimes attended with my wife because his wife would invite us to meet other Hispanics—most of them undocumented. I stopped going when the pastor invited us deer hunting with rifles that disgusted me.

I recall a Georgia state representative defending on one of those radio programs the need to "ban teaching *theories* instead of *facts*." I published some articles about this moment in Mexico's *Milenio* newspaper before they decided (after ten years of weekly contributions) to erase me completely without any explanation, apology, or acknowledgment.

The Georgia representative classified the *theory* of evolution as mere theory. If it's called theory, then it's theory - just as Nazi (National Socialism) is socialism and cabbages grow from eggs. Creationism and the (then) more recent *Intelligent Design* (supported by George Bush) weren't theories but *facts*, recorded in the Bible. The idea that a text should be interpreted in context didn't factor in, especially when atheist French thinkers (Derrida was fashionable in universities then) championed the death of the author, complete interpretative freedom, even a text's inherent emptiness. I wrote what still seems obvious: readers may understand a text however they wish, but writing's purpose is to limit interpretative freedom (see *The Narrative of the Invisible*).

Second obvious point: every belief is also a theory. The difference between the Theory of Creation in seven days and the Theory of Evolution is that one requires no data, no facts, nothing but faith.

Now let me jump twenty Gardelian years to examine the issue from a less epistemological and more psychological perspective - what actually matters in social, political, and media dynamics.

I often begin my Jacksonville University classes with a student presentation, to see how young people understand topics and avoid preconditioning them with my supposed knowledge. Still, they know my stance on global issues from day one. I warn them honestly: "Folks, don't expect neutrality from me. Living in society means committing to certain values - some things are right to me, others wrong. Same for you all."

This doesn't mean facts exist independently of personal opinions, but that every fact is always interpreted by someone. (This also gives dissenters time to drop the course and seek confirmation of their faith elsewhere, like their churches.)

In spring 2024, we discussed Operation Mockingbird (the CIA's hemisphere-wide opinion manipulation program) and how social narratives manipulate facts. My most resisted point was that individuals always vulnerably believe assertions presented as obvious facts by authoritative sources.

No consensus emerged - fine. The class continued with that day's presentation by a student. Moving to the back, I noticed one student dozing off. Minutes later, he was completely *knockout*. When Ingrid finished presenting and classmates applauded, Christian remained asleep. Some athlete students wake at 4 a.m. for gym or rowing on our campus river. With classmates' complicit silence, I placed two chairs on his desk.

Christian woke fifteen minutes later. Discreetly removing the chairs,

"Christian, why'd you put chairs on your desk?" I asked.

He hesitated before answering:

"I wanted some privacy."

"Don't ever put chairs on the desk again," I said. "It's disrespectful."

"Sorry professor," Christian replied. "Won't happen again."

Tense silence filled the room - no laughter or protests - until I explained what really happened and that all his classmates knew. He had accepted without question a fact established by authority, in this case, the professor.

When class ended, Christian was the last to leave.

"I'm sorry," I told him. "I didn't mean to make you feel bad, but to illustrate our earlier discussion."

"On the contrary, professor," Christian said. "You blow my mind. I can't stop thinking that's exactly what we do every day..."

Well, I thought, Christian's attitude was commendable.

I wasn't so sure the rest of society could understand it the same way.

# PRINCIPLES AND RESULTS

According to Donald Trump's voters, the fact that their candidate supports racism and xenophobia are issues that shouldn't distract us from the main goal of first winning the election and then solving those problems.

According to Kamala Harris's voters, the fact that their candidate supports genocide in Gaza, the occupation in Palestine, and bombings in Lebanon are issues that shouldn't distract us from the main goal of first winning the election and then solving those problems.

In U.S. elections (and those of many other countries), we've long grown accustomed to the idea that we must first win elections before following our ideological, ethical, and moral principles. Isn't decent politics supposed to work the other way around? First ethical and moral principles, then results?

Could it be that some portion of voters prioritizes principles over results, and that this margin could decide electoral outcomes, at least once in a lifetime?

I suspect—I'd like to think—yes.

# Syria, Just One More Step Toward Hell

With the swift (and orchestrated) overthrow of Bashar al-Assad, the civil war in Syria, fueled from abroad, hasn't ended. On the contrary, it will enter a new phase as we continue advancing toward total war across the Ring of Fire.

It's a matter of months, maybe weeks, before volunteer fighters regroup with the Syrian army into militias and unleash a chaos that the Washington-Tel Aviv axis—fanatical supremacists skilled in demolition but incapable of building anything—won't control so easily. From the mujahideen, the Taliban, Al Qaeda and ISIS, the "rebels" and "freedom fighters," among others, no Frankenstein created by the West has ever ended well—not even for its own interests.

Meanwhile, China, which is the first and final target of this imperialist offensive, continues to nap in the prosperity of its economic growth, while its allies (Russia, Iran, Yemen, and all the smaller militias resisting in the Ring of Fire) bleed to cover the back of the giant anchored in the Asian continent. Despite its increased military and technological spending, it seems unwilling to see that, in the long run, the geopolitical chessboard may leave it in a less favorable position than the world assumes.

# BLOOD OLYMPICS

The Greek Olympics were capable of interrupting wars to re-spect the sanctity of the sporting event. This truce, practiced since the 8th century B.C., was called *ekecheiria*, under which both ath-letes and spectators from warring nations could travel safely to the host city of the games and return, all under the protection of mutual honor. Athletes and attendees often traveled from what are now Greece, Turkey, Italy, and even North Africa—distances that were longer and more arduous back then than a trip from Tierra del Fuego or Jakarta to Paris is today.

Before becoming another commercial product in our capitalist civilization, the goddess of the Olympic Games was Nike, or *victory*, the cry of Marathon before collapsing dead from heroic exertion. The *ekecheiria*, the truce, the suspension of all wars, was dedicated to Irene (Eirene), the goddess of Peace and sister of Dike, goddess of justice. Greek artists often depicted her as a beautiful young woman holding the child Ploutos in her left arm, even though Ploutos was not her son. Like the Statue of Liberty in New York, Irene also wore a crown and, in her right arm, raised a torch. Before becoming a new myth (the capitalist myth of *freedom of appropriation*), this gesture and the very concept of *freedom* had a very different meaning than it does today—and for thousands of years, it was more or less the same across different cultures and continents: it was the gesture of the generous ruler stepping forward to announce that, at that historical moment, the debts of the oppressed would be forgiven. This gesture was not simply an act of generosity, but an existential necessity for the continued functioning of a stagnant, declining society. Hence the idea of *freedom*, since many slaves and non-slaves were not free due to their debts—exactly as occurs today. As explained by the great American debt economist Michael Hudson, the phrase "*Lord, forgive us our sins*" stems from the oldest and most repeated plea of "lord, forgive our debts," which appears even in the Bible—when translated without the religious dogmas of the time.

The Ploutos held by Irene, goddess of peace, was (or is) the god of wealth, which made sense for the ancient world: prosperity springs from peace. With tragic irony, today's so-called democracies are plutocracies—expressions of the power of the rich, who multiply their wealth with every war. For capitalist investors, the returns on peace are meager and slow.

After 2700 years, we've finally become civilized and things are different. Ploutos grew up and murdered Irene, which explains the abolition of *ekecheiria* in the Olympics and any other major sporting event like the World Cup. In 1992, there was an attempt to revive this ancient tradition, and the United Nations passed a resolution that—like many of its resolutions—only applies when it benefits or doesn't bother the neighborhood bullies.

Now, major sporting events—not just the Olympics—have always been marked by high politics. Some cases from the last century are remembered in history books more for their political betrayals than athletic achievements.

After winning everything, Uruguay refused to participate in the 1934 Italy World Cup in protest of European arrogance that complained Uruguay's first hosted World Cup was too far from the center—which reminds me of the joke my dear father used to make: "*better you come here, since you're closer.*" Uruguay had traveled to Europe for the 1924 Paris and 1928 Amsterdam Olympics, winning both when those tournaments were the true world championships where countries sent their best players, not alternate teams or age-limited squads like today.

By France 1938, Uruguay protested again as Europeans broke their promise of rotating World Cups between continents (the hosting rights belonged to Argentina, where Uruguay remains favored to this day), while also honoring the anti-fascist boycott then led by Hitler and Mussolini. Moreover, Uruguay was the first national team to compete internationally with a Black player—an ethical and political statement that unsettled many, including some Latin American nations.

Unsurprisingly, Italy kept winning World Cups until they were suspended for war, and when tournaments resumed in Brazil, Uruguay claimed victory again with the legendary Maracanazo—a national myth woven into the psychological DNA of that small, sparsely populated country.

Something similar could be said of the 1978 Argentina World Cup. Uruguay abstained not for political reasons but due to failing qualifications—though their refusal to call up overseas stars for qualifiers may have stemmed from their own military dictatorship, but this is just a footnote for football historians.

The '78 World Cup was a gift for genocidal dictator Rafael Videla, who spared no effort pressuring his own players during training sessions, foreign teams (like Peru's), and rushing into victory photos when Argentina secured its first world title—a very different achievement from 1986. It was a political-sporting carnival amid the massacres and disappearances of a fascist regime that used the tournament as Mussolini had the '34 World Cup, Hitler the 1936 Olympics, and FIFA's 1938 World Cup, à la *Die Europa über alles*—Europe above all, Europe first.

Historians will say something similar about the 2024 Paris Olympics. They'll be remembered as the Genocide Olympics, by whatever name. None of the ongoing wars have triggered any *ekecheiria* (truce)—quite the opposite. In the media age, the powerful always await global distractions to commit their worst atrocities. As in the times of Nazism and fascism, the only effect has been to marginalize those not favored by the central political power—like Russia—while inviting Israel to participate amid one of the worst genocides in recent generations. What makes it worse is that this genocide is not only rooted in explicit, unabashed racism (ironically, it's in sports where we see the strongest resistance to racism) but is being committed with the weapons, money, and media blessing of the same hegemonic center that, much like during slavery, beats its chest while proclaiming itself the champion of Democracy, Freedom, and Human Rights.

Three moral categories in which they wouldn't even qualify for a medal—yet they pin them on themselves anyway.

# THE FREEDOM OF THOSE ABOVE

In 2017, Indian-British diplomat and intellectual Shashi Tharoor participated in a panel in Australia. An attendee challenged his position by citing official history: *"According to you, Britain left India worse off than it found it... What about the engineering skills, infrastructure, and above all, the education Indians gained thanks to England?"* Tharoor's response can be summarized in a few sentences: *"The British arrived in one of the richest countries in the world—a nation whose GDP accounted for 27 percent of global wealth in the 18th century and 23 percent in the 19th. After 200 years of plunder and destruction, India was reduced to poverty. When the British left India in 1947, the country represented just 3 percent of the world's GDP, with 90 percent of its population below the poverty line, a literacy rate of 17 percent, and a life expectancy of 27 years. The institutes of technology that exist today were established in India after independence (...) India had been the world's largest textile producer for two thousand years... The classic excuse is: 'Oh, it's not our fault you missed the Industrial Revolution train.' Of course we missed the train; it's because you pushed us under its wheels. In the name of the 'free market,' the British destroyed at gunpoint the free market that already existed in India".*[i]

In 2022, professors Jason Hickel and Dylan Sullivan published a detailed analysis titled *"Capitalism and extreme poverty"* where they calculate the impact of capitalism's imperial policies. In India alone, within just forty years, British colonialism caused over 100 million deaths and stole at least 45 trillion dollars in goods—that is, more than ten times the current economy of the entire United Kingdom. By analyzing three basic quantitative factors (real wages, physical stature, and mortality), the researchers demolished the notion that before capitalism's reign, 90 percent of the population lived in extreme poverty, and that capitalism was precisely the system that created global wealth. This popular prejudice could only apply to imperialist countries, not the rest of the world. *"The rise of capitalism caused a dramatic deterioration in human well-being. In all regions studied, incorporation into the capitalist world system was associated with wages falling below subsistence levels, a decline in human stature, and a spike in premature mortality. In parts of South Asia, sub-Saharan Africa, and Latin America, well-being levels still haven't recovered. Where progress has occurred, significant improvements in human well-being began several centuries after capitalism's emergence. In core regions of Northwestern Europe, progress began in the 1880s, while in the periphery it started in the mid-20th century—a period characterized by the rise of socialist and anti-colonial political movements that redistributed income and established public provisioning systems"*.[ii] In an article published in *New Internationalist*, the same authors summarize their earlier study as follows: in the 20th century, *"the amount of food an average worker's wages could buy in Latin America and much of sub-Saharan Africa decreased significantly, reaching levels lower than those of the 17th and 18th centuries"*. Regarding the last 50 years, they conclude that, following the backlash against social and progressive movements in the Global North *"neoliberal policy was implemented by corporate-aligned governments, most notably those of Margaret Thatcher and Ronald Reagan. In the Global South, it was often implemented through coups and other violent imperialist interventions by the U.S. and its allies, including in countries like Indonesia (1965), Chile (1973), Burkina Faso (1987), and Iraq (2003). The IMF and World Bank imposed neoliberal ideology on countries not subjected to invasions and coups through 'Structural Adjustment Programs' (SAPs), which required governments to*

*privatize national resources and public goods, slash labor and environ-*
*mental protections, restrict public services, and most crucially, eliminate*
*programs aimed at ensuring universal access to food and other essential*
*goods. Between 1981 and 2004, 123 countries (82 percent of the world's*
*population) were forced to implement SAPs. Economic policy for most of*
*humanity came to be determined by bankers and technocrats in Washing-*
*ton".*[iii] It's worth clarifying that the so-called "Global South,"
though dominated by oceans on world maps, isn't just the area
south of the equator but extends from Latin America, Africa, and
Asia far northward—representing by far the majority of the world's
population. But international banks operate like any corporation.
At the IMF, 85 percent of the world's population holds just 45 percent of the votes; as in any corporate boardroom, more money
means more votes. Essentially, like any hijacked democracy. American democracy itself emerged under similar constraints, designed to
ensure ordinary people (non-white and without major property
holdings) couldn't wield real decision-making power.

This kind of fact-based, documented historical analysis is always
dismissed as exaggerated, radical, and even condemned or banned.
Yet beyond being courageous, it's correct. As Karl Marx explained
in *Capital*, wealth and capital aren't the same thing, though both
tend toward accumulation. Capitalism (the system and culture surrounding capital) demanded the *reinvestment of surplus value* and the
maximization of labor, detached (*alienated*) from the produced ob-
ject and, as was the initial case in England, dispossessed of their land
so their children would become wage workers. *"The separation of la-*
*bor from its product, the separation of subjective labor power from its ob-*
*jective conditions, was the real foundation and starting point of capitalist*
*production. [...] The worker therefore constantly produces material*
*wealth—objective wealth—but in the form of capital, that is, as an alien*

*power that dominates and exploits them.*"[iv] Over a hundred pages later: "*Today, industrial supremacy implies commercial supremacy. [...] The creation of surplus value has become humanity's sole objective.*" Later, with an irony that resonates today, Marx observes that "*the only part of so-called* national wealth *that truly belongs to the* collective possessions *of modern citizens is their* national debt.*"*

This frenetic European process interrupted economic and civilizational development in other parts of the world, from the Americas to Asia. One might ask whether this imposition of a new culture following feudalism could have succeeded without a strong degree of fanaticism. I believe not, as with any other historical moment. (Collective) fanaticism is a fundamental component of all geopolitical and historical success, be it feudal wars, capitalism's imperial wars, or 20th-century communism's conflicts. The victor will impose their interests, their values, and create a new worldview—that is, a new normal—which even their victims will defend with passion and conviction.

By the mid-19th century, Marx noted: "*The colonial system, with its public debts, heavy taxes, protectionism, and trade wars, emerged from the manufacturing revolution. All of which grew enormously during modern industry's infancy. The consequence is a great slaughter of innocents.*" Later he adds: "*The American Civil War brought a colossal national debt and, with it, heavy tax pressure and the rise of a vile financial aristocracy [...] In short, an accelerated concentration of capital. In other words, the great American republic has ceased to be the promised land for migrant workers.*"

# We WILL RULE OVER THE ASHES, OR BECOME ASHES OURSELVES

On September 4, 2024, a tropical storm hit Jacksonville. The conversation with Jill Stein in the university auditorium was scheduled for 5:30 PM, by which time the storm had turned day into pitch-black night. To reduce our audience (this is my speculation), the Florida Democratic Party Committee had decided to organize a speech by Kamala Harris's Senate candidates on the same campus, at Jacksonville University's College of Business, one hour earlier—when there was barely any parking left.

At the end of the conversation, someone from the audience complained that I had been "too kind" to Stein. On the way out, I recognized them as a Democratic voter, a decent person from what I'd seen.

"I'm not a journalist," I told them. "The idea here was to delve deeper into Stein's ideas."

Truthfully, I dislike the star-making game, the Univision Jorge Ramos approach of harassing interviewees. Perhaps that's why I always considered Spain's Jesús Quintero a master of the genre, with his interviews full of near-psychoanalytic silences.

From the auditorium, we went to share a modest dinner in a museum hall nearby, reserved by my colleagues to thank Jill, former Congressman and Green Party coordinator Jason Call, and their team for making the effort to come.

The austere dinner had been left there by the university catering service. With no waitstaff and no audience, my colleagues and I could share an interesting conversation I won't detail, as it occurred in a private space. But I believe I can connect one thought to both the elections and the global tragedy we're sinking deeper into each day.

I mentioned to Jill, seated beside me, that years earlier I'd been at Deutsche Welle in Berlin where the lead journalist I dined with after the event mentioned being married to Germany's Green Party leader Cem Özdemir—then a congressman and now Germany's Agriculture Minister. Özdemir accepted my invitation to lecture at JU in late 2019, but German police uncovered a plot by the U.S. branch of the century's most violent neo-Nazi group, Atomwaffen Division (AWD), to assassinate him, thwarting the trip.

That was our common ground. But Jill noted a key difference between the U.S. and German Green Parties: Ukraine.

That's as far as my indiscretion goes. I can add that Stein's assessment and position on the issue align completely with mine. There I can elaborate further, to clarify what Stein said that night.

When President Biden withdrew U.S. troops from Afghanistan, he left behind millions in tanks and military hardware during the chaotic retreat. After twenty years of occupation—after nearly a decade of having (supposedly) found and executed Osama bin Laden—suddenly the U.S. military was fleeing as hastily as from Vietnam. After twenty years, Americans lost $14 trillion (seven Brazils' worth) in Afghanistan alone—not building schools and hospitals, but funding a military domination project that only benefited drug trafficking and private companies, as the Wall Street Journal exposed.

After 20 years, Washington left Afghanistan's government in the hands of the CIA's prodigal sons, the Taliban, after eliminating another of their prodigal sons, Osama bin Laden. A perfect business model: create more problems to invest in new military solutions.

As we've said before, part of America's historic failures in wars beyond mere airstrikes stems not just from inefficiency, but because losing wars is big business for the private corporations dominating U.S. politics and narratives. Back then, we warned in an article to just wait for a new war—that this mysterious retreat only made sense as urgency for a new plan underway.

Then came Russia's invasion of Ukraine. Earlier, many agreed everything possible had been done to provoke it, getting Zelensky (Washington's puppet, a clown by profession) to confirm Ukraine's NATO membership process. NATO—Hitler's dream (two of its directors were Hitler's aides)—once again achieved its goal of escalating tensions to extend the hegemony of the Alpha Male, the Anglo-Saxon West, something that began right after WWII and could've been resolved by Stalin's 1952 proposal, known as the "Stalin notes."

In March 2022, *Le Monde* in Paris published a page describing Paco Ignacio Taibo II and me as *"leftist intellectuals pro-Putin,"* despite the fact that before and after that report I never missed an opportunity to make clear that while I didn't approve of the invasion, I considered it criminal hypocrisy to attempt writing history starting from that day without considering the prolonged harassment, the massacres of Russian-speaking populations in Donbas, and the coup against democratically elected president Viktor Yanukovych promoted by the West.

I'm not "pro-anyone" but "pro-causes," like the cause of Non-Interference by one country in another's policies—as if it were some cowboy-and-Indian problem where aggressors always portray themselves as victims of reaction. The old and persistent interventionisms, mother of all problems in Global South countries... This was essentially our shared view that night of September 4.

On November 1, a statement from Europe's Greens urged Jill Stein to withdraw from the election and support Kamala Harris to prevent a fascist Trump government. *"Jill Stein and the U.S. Green*

*Party aren't affiliated with the Global Greens... All who support 'green principles' should vote for Kamala Harris,"* declared Finnish congressman Oras Tynkkynen. They're worried about the chaos they created in Ukraine, not the genocide they're perpetrating in Palestine.

Democrats have insisted on blaming Jill Stein for a potential defeat, yet *they've done nothing* to prevent electoral suicide, expressly ignoring demands from millions of furious Democrats over the genocide in Palestine. Whenever Kamala Harris has been challenged at her political rallies, she's silenced protesters by saying *"I'm speaking now,"* then continuing with what sounds like a memorized script: *"yes, it's an important issue, but right now I'm here to discuss other important matters like grocery prices."*

More insensitive hypocrisy and arrogance would be hard to imagine. To top it off, her husband happily announced they'd place a *mezuzah* at the White House entrance—which would be unremarkable in a private residence if not for the timing and location. Then Bill Clinton tried calming Gaza protests by claiming Israel has special rights because King David was there 3,000 years ago.

So, dear Democrats, stop crying about impending national fascism when you're the primary architects of global fascism.

# westerners, westernizers, and psychowesternism

What's been called "the West" since the Renaissance was for over a millennium just a vague, deeply contradictory idea from the world's most violent continent. The tribal mind needs allies and enemies in a perpetual binary division of the world (us vs. them, Good vs. Evil), like some sports tournament. Flags, symbols, and myths expanded tribal barbarism into grander fantasies called chosen peoples, superior races, and civilized nations.

The modern West didn't form with ancient Greeks or Rome's fall. It emerged with capitalist imperialism in the 16th century, radicalized by Protestantism, gold fever, and the sociopathy of perpetual conquest—subjugating "inferior" peoples while obliging the world's salvation through our ideas, our superstitions, our financial and police power, eliminating any alternative worldview. It's grounded in supremacist fanaticism that neither lives nor lets live.

The reaction of this fantasy called "the West" (today NATO) to its greatest existential crisis in modern history has been to trample all its sermons (equality, freedom, democracy, human rights), revealing its true face: if we can't prevail through propaganda, finance, or economic harassment, we'll do it by cannon fire.

This is precisely how capitalist West emerged: in the name of market freedom, they destroyed the market freedom of what was then the First World (India, Bangladesh, and China), imposing their rules through cannon fire, corruption (which instigated fratricidal wars like in India), and drug addiction like opium in China. In India, they took advantage of a caste system more radical than Europe's Middle Ages, creating collaborating elites above and collaborators below. A tradition that continues today. Just look at the politicians in England and the United States.

According to Jacob Helberg, national security expert and foreign policy advisor to Palantir: "Ukraine is the opportunity to fulfill Palantir Technologies' mission: defend the West and screw our enemies." Enemies. For Palantir CEOs like Karp, there's a *moral imperative* to provide Western governments with the best emerging technology. For this noble reason, *"states must collaborate more with the tech sector"*—meaning private corporations. Palantir's other owner, Peter Thiel, naturally expresses the old Western fixation: *"Unlike the physical world, in cybersecurity it's very easy to attack and very hard to defend."* So let's focus on the former (the old "preemptive strike"), since human existence is defined by conflict and war, and the solution isn't peace or negotiation but the *extermination* of the adversary.

For psychowesternism, there's no room for two "alpha males"— another of the New Right's central metaphors expressing Europe's old obsession; if we win and dictate, the world is at peace. As with mega-businesses, *competition* means *exterminating* the competitor. An alternative vision would be negotiation for common good, as small businesses do, as humans cooperate when not sick with this individualism psychopathy.

This is why China is seen as the enemy to destroy, just as it was destroyed in the Opium Wars. Though the strategy has been to first demonize and harass the great region surrounding it (Russia-Iran) through its main bastions (Ukraine-Israel-India-Taiwan), politicians no longer hide that China is the real target. Why? Because it has an *excessively* successful economy and, though it hasn't fired a single shot to become the world's leading power (the opposite of how capitalist West was built and maintained), its mere success—unaligned with our interests—defines it as *our enemy*, the Empire of Evil. Needless to say, this is the most direct path to war with China, which won't wait until the last moment to invest tons of capital in its military complex and more nuclear bombs.

Like so many other U.S. generals and congressmen, Mike Gallagher took a position as defense business director at Palantir. The same Gallagher published an article in May 2024 in *Foreign Affairs* titled *"No Substitute for Victory: America's Competition With China Must Be Won, Not Managed,"* arguing that Washington must *"rearm the U.S. military to reduce China's economic influence"* and counter its *"malevolent strategy..."* John Wayne-style psychowesternism.

The Quincy Institute, considering the sinophobia of Gallagher and Karp (Palantir's CEO), warned we're heading toward war with China. It doesn't clarify that we're the ones who've decided to march into that violent scenario—which will bring huge profits (economic and political) to companies like Palantir while plunging the rest of the world into total crisis, especially the West. A war over Taiwan is the West's desired scenario, but it might be cheaper and more strategic to invent a war between China and India over Kashmir... Well, better not give them ideas.

Warming up to the idea, VP candidate J.D. Vance said countering China will be a foreign policy priority for Donald Trump—a script seemingly handed to him by better-prepared, more informed, and powerful people than the apprentice Vance, friend of Palantir's millionaires and other tech moguls, his main donors.

The American empire can no longer rely on dollar imposition, so it must leverage AI-equipped weapons, already being tested in Ukraine and Palestine. In 2024, Israel's Ministry of Defense reached an agreement with Thiel and Karp to *"leverage Palantir's advanced technology in support of war-related missions"*. If in the past they experimented with drugs and syphilis in Latin America, now they're testing the effectiveness of all this intelligence advancement to ruthlessly eliminate men, children, and women—demonstrating new weapons' efficiency and their impact on public opinion, which they calculate will cease to matter because part of the plan involves eliminating the inconvenient elections of dysfunctional liberal democracies—see our analysis of Curtis Yarvin.

It's the old Western mentality that now, unmasked, we see in Israel massacring without limits because "only we matter," "others are savages," "we're the superior race and must be obeyed," plus "we're God's chosen people" with a "manifest destiny." Others' lives hold no value. The only thing that matters is winning, at any cost.

Now, experience shows all this multimillion-dollar super technology provides great military advantage but isn't delivering expected results. Not in Ukraine, not in Palestine, nor in the rest of the monitored and manipulated world. One of High Tech's Achilles' heels is Low Tech—the less sophisticated the technology, the harder to control or predict its users. Hence the resort to brute-force bombardment, like Israel's.

World War III, the final World War, is Plan A. We must imagine a Plan B and rally all powerless forces to resist the psychopaths and merchants of death.

# WORLD WAR III ON THE DRAWING BOARD

As with every sunset in Colonia del Sacramento, I sat beneath my grandparents' olive trees, resting after a long day harvesting tomatoes at the farm, with my then-beloved *Universal History of Art* by José Ráfols on my lap. Someone (I think one of my uncles, though I couldn't see his face) approached and said I wasn't properly explaining the problem because I wasn't asking the right question.

I woke unsettled, still thinking about the same problem that had exhausted me the previous day. I understood what that unknown uncle meant—perhaps the uncle who died in a mysterious accident forty years ago. At first it seemed an irrelevant problem: the same global circus produced in a powerful nation's government house. But the missing question came with a tragic answer.

I'll try to explain.

### The Missing Question
Discussions about Trump administration policies revolve around potential consequences of tariff measures that have shaken half the world: stock markets, inflation, reindustrialization, "prosperity never seen before." All stem from presidential decrees and declarations of intent.

Something's absent from dominant media and academic analyses—not the consequences or stated intentions, but the *origin* of it all. Not a historical origin, but its opposite. A teleological origin, a cause precariously located in the future.

Approaching it this way reveals not just consistency between the tariff frenzy and other administration policies (like the war on immigration and universities), but also a dramatic conclusion.

First, I'll summarize the (significant) contradictions in these policies and narratives.

### Tariffs

The U.S. has a trade deficit and real debt—though not as severe as Japan's. Business geniuses have always built success, gunpoint-enforced, on personal irresponsibility and others' obligations. An old trick, but like all crises, used as smokescreen to squeeze those below.

In theory, tariffs would balance financial accounts, but actual measures reveal something hard to dismiss as ignorance. As economists know, we all run deficits with our grocery stores and surpluses with employers. Yet April 2025's announced plan ("Liberation Day") proposed blanket tariffs on practically the entire world.

In 1890 McKinley caused the century's worst recession with tariff policies. In 1930, President Hoover worsened the crisis with more tariffs, triggering the 1930s Great Depression that forced the nation to socialize its way out of catastrophe. A central factor in that crisis predicted by Marx and initiated in 1929 with Wall Street's collapse was the overproduction of industrial goods that couldn't be sold because workers lacked purchasing power.

Now, let's bring these historical lessons to the present and imagine a miracle occurs—the United States reindustrializes with wages no one would accept today. Who will buy the industrial products that our middle class can't afford, nor can 96% of the world due to tariff barriers?

## Savings

The Real Objective requires this servile, unconditional working class in perpetual need. To achieve this, their political rights (like free speech) and social benefits—created by Roosevelt in the 30s and Johnson in the 60s, then eroded by the neoliberal wave since Reagan-Thatcher—must be radically dismantled: public education, state health programs like Medicare and Medicaid.

What better for a suffering population, dulled by politico-religious propaganda, than more circus? Elon Musk's chainsaw is one such clownish prop that Argentine president Javier Milei didn't invent—a neoliberal Uruguayan president, Lacalle Herrera, already used it in the 90s. This chainsaw (DOGE) has already destroyed hundreds of thousands of jobs without achieving its goals. Instead, its destructive machinery saved $150 billion while, through sheer bureaucratic inefficiency, created $130 billion in deadweight loss, further eroding production and consumption.

Let's not forget that beyond the Anglo-Saxon fanaticism hidden behind patriotic excuses, these policies are written by a government of the rich, by the rich, and for the rich. The top 1% of Americans own $50 trillion—double the U.S. GDP.

But we must "save" by stripping medical assistance from poor retirees. They're neither productive nor will fight any wars.

## Immigration

Trump's indiscriminate deportation policies and racist rhetoric are both personal additions and cultural staples of this country. They're part of the circus and classic fascist incitement, but also align with the Real Objective. Those millions of highly productive workers (and consumers) could be legalized, as Reagan did in 1986, but the Real Objective distrusts the unconditional submission of non-

Caucasian foreigners. (Recall that beyond the trillions superpowers invest in Intelligence analysis, everything boils down to the limited intellect of a small group of psychopaths with rather mediocre IQs. Someone slightly better connected told me they hate me for this "arrogance"—and frankly, I couldn't care less.)

The stated purpose isn't their Black or mixed heritage, but crime reduction, while creating manufacturing jobs for citizens. A contradiction by any measure. Currently, half a million industrial jobs remain perpetually vacant, a number growing daily. Since Hispanics can't be called unproductive, they're branded murderers and rapists, despite their crime rates being far below nationals'.

The traditional excuse was "We're not against immigration, just illegal immigration" (see "Racism Doesn't Need Racists"). Now, as these racist/xenophobic arguments prove insufficient for the Real Objective, they're criminalizing legal immigrants: foreign professors and students, all documented, using two unconstitutional excuses: (1) expel, demoralize, discredit, or silence critics of Israel by branding them antisemites; (2) Chinese are communists by birth, thus threats to America. And Nazis? Well, welcome as always.

### Universities

It's the same labor base problem, but at the pyramid's peak: any reindustrialization, already difficult due to domestic wages, becomes doubly impossible through these very measures. Reindustrialization requires universities, science, technology. Yet for the Real Objective, per VP Vance: "Professors are the enemy," and for Project 2025: "Universities are the enemy." When Eugene Debs and other anti-imperialist Americans spoke against entering WWI, they were jailed for the "crime of opinion." Now, a century later, as I explained in $P = d.t$, when power trembles, tolerance for diversity-dissent-democracy decreases proportionally.

Though the rhetoric focuses on "only Americans matter," even American students don't want to attend universities without international students. Why? Because of the now-dangerous diversity. Because they're not stupid. Students know that diversity of experiences and perspectives drives scientific and academic progress across all fields. Moreover, they understand that to build careers beyond mere animal survival, they must network with people worldwide—even if they never bother traveling abroad.

Years ago, I visited MIT at Noam Chomsky's invitation for a discussion. Walking through its buildings, I encountered an overwhelming majority of students and professors speaking various languages or English with foreign accents. The same holds for Harvard and nearly every reputable university. For decades, most U.S. patents have been created by foreigners. Precisely this surviving advantage is what the architects of Project 2025 and the Real Objective aim to destroy.

### The Real Objective

Trump's obsession with impossible reindustrialization using 1960s-era wages conceals a global problem and a dark warning: *the goal is to make America self-sufficient in preparation for global war.*

Why must we reach this extreme? For the reason we've elaborated for years: unlike other cultures and continents, the Northwest only developed through imperial brutality and the power to erase others' prosperity while preaching the opposite. Specifically, the Protestant Anglo-Saxon world cannot perceive anything or anyone without classifying them as angel or demon. Naturally, the demons (savages, terrorists) are always others—and eliminating them becomes urgent before they entertain the same idea.

This Real Objective (undoubtedly gracing some mahogany desk under a more poetic name) anticipates and promotes World War III based on concrete data from current battlefields. It would insult humanity's innocence to dismiss this hypothesis—which I consider our greatest crisis since 850,000 BC, when only 1,200 humans survived globally for reasons scientists still investigate.

World War II didn't just boost U.S. industry—it cemented Anglo-Saxon hegemony amid Britain's decline. The postwar era (the Cold War) proved the Northwest Empire's (NATO's) efficacy through aggression and harassment, not negotiation or coexistence.

Two key case studies now occupy those mahogany desks:

## I

Russia is the most feared—and desired—example. Notes and debates about Russia must be raging now, as they offer an irrefutable surprise test: a mid-sized nation enduring prolonged warfare under NATO's unified blockade and harassment without economic collapse—quite the opposite. The key wasn't just technological prowess (still inferior to America's) but its *industrial and agricultural self-sufficiency*.

White House spokeswoman Karoline Leavitt declared: "We need more plumbers and fewer cultural studies graduates." These recycled ideas don't just follow the fascist playbook by fabricating false dichotomies to keep the lower classes divided—they serve a dual purpose: (1) A plumber who never hears systemic critiques will remain obedient while blaming critics for his plight, and (2) for the Real Objective, functional slaves become crucial, as there won't be enough prisons for saboteurs like Eugene Debs.

**II**

Gaza is the other laboratory where this Anglo-Zionist psyche—psychopathic beyond comprehension—studies global reactions to surreal massacres and how outrage, protests, and public opinion are controlled.

Volumes have been written on this vast topic. Space prevents revisiting details here, but I believe the explanation for this darkness has been made sufficiently clear.

# APPENDICES

## WITH THE ELITES GETTING NERVOUS

When in December 2024 the CEO of UnitedHealthcare was reported murdered on a New York street en route to an investor convention, media outlets endlessly commented on the brutal crime against an important person. Soon after, a phenomenon occurred that made millionaire CEOs like Brian Thompson nervous and bewildered everyone else. The killer became a sort of avenging Zorro. When it was revealed that the bullet that killed him bore the inscription *Delay, Deny, Defend*, all doubts vanished. The assassin had acted in revenge against the most notorious and hated practice of healthcare lobby mafias that present themselves as the "health insurance industry"—a triple oxymoron.

UnitedHealth Group alone is valued at $500 trillion—more than Colombia's entire economy. Its healthcare record is questionable. Back in 2009, a Harvard University study had concluded that "45,000 people die annually because of the private health insurance industry." This is what happens when a basic need ceases to be a right and becomes a business, a commodity that impoverishes an entire nation while enriching less than one percent.

The unexpected popular reaction—which has precedents in another era of obscene social inequality (the Gilded Age before the late 19th century Great Recession)—unnerved many. The justice system reacted just as it had then: they charged Luigi Mangione not with murder, but with *terrorism*. All periods of millionaire excess have been accompanied by this kind of violence and ended in social ruptures.

None of these past orgies compares to the present one. Though Elon Musk was never elected by anyone, his fortune has bought not only mass-manipulation media like Twitter but also presidents like Trump, to whom he donated $250 million for his electoral campaign. Trump repaid him with an extreme political and social power position in government, in addition to what he already wielded through his CIA-backed satellite company. From the heights of this power (and during his drug-fueled nights), Musk—the son of South African apartheid, America's most dangerous immigrant, now named Head of the Department of Government Efficiency in the incoming administration—has proposed two solutions for the country's problems: deport poor (non-white) immigrants and slash social security for the working class.

One step closer to the Great Rupture. Economic crises are capitalism's invention (previously caused by external factors), but it's fair to suspect they're also part of the plan to plunder the working classes. Economic crises are major investments for millionaires (the only true capitalists), allowing them to buy everything at desperation prices—which explains why after initial losses, they multiply their capital and political power within a decade. Until they overplay their hand, as in 1929, creating not just a crisis but a depression that typically rouses the lower classes and forces political and ideological changes later labeled *radical*.

Radical? A U.S. construction worker laboring five days a week—under summer sun and winter snow—would need 45 million years to save the fortune Elon Musk amassed in under twenty years. That's if they never go into debt first. Forty-five million years ago, the Himalayas didn't exist yet. The landmass of India was just beginning to collide with Asia, and over 44 million years remained before Homo sapiens would walk the African continent.

The system producing all this ideological pornography isn't new. It's the same one that existed exactly a century ago in Europe and America: a fierce persecution by the oligarchy's propaganda machinery against traditional workers' organizations and demands for social security. In America a hundred years ago, labor unions and even part of the (Irish) Catholic Church had won public opinion over the need for minimum wage, unemployment insurance, and banning child labor.

A century ago, social disparities promoted from Wall Street (the greatest capital accumulation center since slavery) were beginning to hit historic peaks. On both sides of the North Atlantic, fascism started seducing dissatisfied masses who felt the problem and their frustrations but didn't understand them. It all ended in the way history knows best. A radical rupture. In this case, it was an economic catastrophe that exacerbated conditions of poverty and social injustice.

Until F.D. Roosevelt implemented what is supposedly the primary way to prevent these problems: the establishment of social policies (socialist, according to critics of the time), such as creating Social Security, subsidies for the underprivileged, recognizing the right to strike, and fierce state intervention in the economy through public works. It worked, though the system that had caused the catastrophe survived. The exact opposite of the neocolonial austerity recommendations ("economic adjustment") prescribed by the IMF.

Europe proceeded similarly, with heavy state interventions— from Nazi Germany to the communist Soviet Union. In both cases, it resulted in overwhelming economic success, though the rest of the story wasn't equally brilliant. The U.S. and England had to swallow their sympathies for Hitler and ally with Stalin, especially when the Soviet Union began showing signs of a lightning counteroffensive against the German invasion.

The obsessions of the capitalist system, now unchecked, are repeating with the same features as a century ago. But since we're cavemen with greater technological power, we learn nothing from history or our own monsters because each generation tends to forget—not only history but the pain of grandparents who endured national and global traumas. Each generation believes itself at the pinnacle of understanding and underestimates its predecessors, without even considering that nearly all our super-technology was invented by earlier generations. New generations grow insensitive to their grandparents' tragedies—especially when disdain for education, knowledge, culture, and critical thinking is in fashion.

Could it be that history's pendulum changes direction every three generations? That every generation that values civility, solidarity, and empathy is preceded by one that suffered their destruction, which in turn was preceded by one that scorned them?

We seem to be in this generation of contempt, proudly upholding capitalism's most perverse historical myth: *"the unfettered selfishness of the individual benefits society."* A society-archipelago of alienated islands. A generation that will be followed by crisis, fascism, and rebellion from below.

How is it possible that most people adopt, with such passion and conviction, the ideas of a minority? Karl Marx gave the answer in the 19th century: *"The ideas of the ruling class are the ruling ideas of every epoch."* The ruling class, though it may not even constitute one percent of society—as is the case today—not only owns (has appropriated) the means of production and all of humanity's inventions over centuries, but also controls the means of financing, political power, and communication. This has been true since Ancient Rome, from the sermons of priests interpreting the Bible for illiterate congregations in cathedrals financed by feudal lords, to their heirs—the liberals—who seized the printing press, then radio, then television, then the internet, then social media, then artificial intelligence...

One thing is clear: this system has no future. Its strategy is to prolong the agony of those below and the champagne of those above for as long as possible.

# TrUMP II anD THe years To come

Trump II and the years to come December 27, 2024
*Interview with Jorge Majfud*
*By Gerard Yong, journalist, Mexico*

*Facing a new Donald Trump presidency—one that seems to have be-*
*gun before reentering the Oval Office—we spoke with Jorge Majfud to*
*understand how we reached this moment in the U.S. and the world, what*
*Latin America can expect, and what lies ahead in the coming years.*

**GY: Could we say that, given the prospect of annexing Mex-
ico and Canada into the U.S., we're seeing a new economic
model more consistent with a system of annexation rather than
open globalization?**

JM: That would be the final stage of this new Cold War with
China, which has already crossed some boundaries of the previous
Cold War—though back then, Vietnam was what Ukraine and Palestine are today for the West, while Africa and Latin America are
beginning to resemble their roles in that chessboard: independence
movements infiltrated by Trojan horses. The same movements, the
same strategy: dominate the central squares by sacrificing some
pawns before executing a checkmate maneuver.

**GY: But the fantasy of invasion always lingers...**

JM: Without a doubt. Many hawks in the U.S. Senate would love
to invade Mexico—but not annex it. Mexico is a country too populated by "an inferior race," "a race of corrupt hybrids." When the
U.S. annexed over half of Mexico, they stopped at the Rio Grande

despite having captured the capital precisely to avoid incorporating millions of inferior beings into the Union. For the same reason, they didn't take the entire Caribbean. Many now speak of Canada as "the 51st State," just as when the U.S. was founded with thirteen Anglo-Saxon colonies, they tried to annex Canada as the fourteenth. Not just to escape the curse of the number thirteen, but because Canadians were white Europeans. They failed after several sabotage attempts, and Britain retaliated by burning down the White House in Washington (which wasn't white until then—they painted it to cover the shame).

These new annexations, following the 19th-century imperialist style before shifting to the strategy of global military bases, might see a revival that creates desired crises. But they're unlikely to materialize in the medium term. In the long run (perhaps in two or three generations), the opposite is more probable: the U.S. losing states like Texas or California to secession, or Alaska to Chinese annexation, for example.

**GY: What kind of policies do you expect from Donald Trump toward Mexico in his second term?**

JM: After Mexico's brutal dispossession in another fabricated war in 1846—using the old false-flag attack method and victimizing the aggressor—Mexico's morale sank so low that its leaders (with exceptions) dedicated themselves to handing over the rest to U.S. corporations. The Mexican Revolution changed many things. When Wilson bombed Veracruz, it was its inhabitants who resisted and repelled a months-long occupation. The soldiers retreated. The Mexican Revolution bled Mexico dry but left behind an experience of armed resistance that (I suspect, like other rare cases on the continent) made Washington hesitate to intervene as it once did, with cannon fire and banana-republic coups. This is likely why Lázaro

Cárdenas achieved the unthinkable: nationalizing Mexican oil (perhaps also due to his strategic ambiguity toward European powers).

For these historical reasons, I don't believe Trump or his hawks would dare direct aggression or intervention in Mexico. However, we should expect a far more aggressive presidency than his first for four reasons: 1. Trump won't be running for reelection (at least under the current constitution). 2. Like an addict, his ego needs to leave a mark on history (what they call a "legacy"), whatever it may be. 3. The new right is now openly anti-democratic, no longer hiding it, and their ideology—though elementary and primitive (Alpha Male mentality)—fuels aggression, whether between individuals or nations. 4. The U.S. is an empire in economic, social, political, and geopolitical decline, making it even more aggressive.

Mexico has always occupied a unique position, different from the rest of Latin America. It is both vulnerable and strong. Like in Cárdenas' time, it must forge economic alliances with various powers like China (since joining BRICS+ is unlikely soon) and regional alliances across Latin America. Alliances and unions are the only viable path to independence—an indispensable condition for development in countries that aren't micro-colonies.

**GY: Some believe Trump could negotiate with Russia for a peaceful exit to the Ukraine war, possibly to Ukraine's detriment... What are your thoughts?**

JM: His ego could play a positive role in ending the Ukraine war through negotiation. Trump relates to strongmen—not because he is one, but because they're his alter egos. Great leaders aren't egomaniacs, but power-seekers are, and Trump (like Musk and others with the same pathology) fits this psychological type perfectly.

On the other hand, we mustn't forget that individuals—elected presidents in a liberal democracy—aren't the power but its mask.

Power lies with those who amass mountains of money (this is neither metaphor nor hyperbole) and, as a direct and indirect result,
buy politicians, media, and the public opinion of majorities who
idolize their enslavers. If we add to this that the most lucrative industry is the death industry, we can only expect that if the big business of war in Ukraine ends, all that capital investment will move to
other regions. Palestine is one case. Syria is another. The most dramatic scenario would be (and this is the intention) continuing with
Iran until reaching Taiwan, thereby expanding the Ring of Fire
we've been discussing for years.

**GY: Are we far from that Ring of Fire?**

JM: Only geographically. Latin America will not face easy times.
Although in the last decade imperial neo-interventionism has operated through media sermons and social networks (still largely controlled by U.S. corporations), it's reasonable to foresee an escalation
of conflict into its CIA-Mossad phase (like during the Cold War)
and then toward a military phase (as during the Banana Wars).

Trump's recent rhetoric about reclaiming the Panama Canal and
annexing Canada and Greenland is an attempt to gradually accli-
mate Americans to normalizing what was once laughable.

**YG: How did we get here?**

JM: In a very simple way. The feudal nobles changed masks once
again. First they became the liberals of pirate companies, like the
East India Company... They were slavers, they were democrats (as
pirates were), and they became neoliberals to continue vampirizing
their colonies and those below them in their own countries. More
recently, with the Soviet Union's suicide, they made the Western left
go vegan by adopting the right's economic ideology: neoliberalism.
As a final blow, the left forgot about class struggle and reduced itself
to a simplistic identity politics—which is also the racist and sexist

politics of the right, but inverted; just, in our view, yet insufficient and a perfect distraction. Once neoliberalism systematically fails decade after decade, leaving decay and debt everywhere—in the colonies and even in the empire itself—the right leaps forward, calls itself *libertarian* and promises the frustrated and enraged masses (facing the obscene results of the capital super-accumulation they themselves created) a magical solution once more. How? By offering more of the same but radically, no longer within liberal democracies but through an undisguised fascism that, as a century ago, promises to satisfy a brutalized people's frustrations—by increasing the drug dosage. Add to this the internal and external collapse of an entire empire and the primitive simplicity of the far right (the tribe, the totem, the race, the fear of the other, rage, and pride), and the picture couldn't be clearer. In short: the right has managed to sell the illusion of a radical solution to problems created by the right, while the left lost its critical and revolutionary mystique by identifying with the right's neoliberal ideology.

# Union and Independence

## Panama Canal: How to Respond to an Aggressor and Be Independent Once and For All. Interview with Jorge Majfud

*"As always, the solution was to intervene in a foreign country, invent a new nation, and then have the Panamanian 'rebels' sign a treaty with a gun to their heads—as was and remains customary."*

Desacato, Brazil: *Since assuming his second term as leader of the White House, Donald Trump has demonstrated his new credentials as a global aggressor. This has been evident with border nations like Mexico and Canada, as well as with China, the Palestinian people, and the Isthmus of Panama—stolen from Colombia to create a country serving imperialist interests.*

*Trump has complained that China is the canal's biggest beneficiary; he demands the U.S. pay less for its ships' transit and even return to administering the canal as it did before the Torrijos-Carter Treaties took effect.*

*But is there anything legitimate or legal about Trump's claims? What is the true history of the canal and the Panamanian isthmus? Is Panama a fully sovereign nation? How does this situation affect other countries in the region?*

*This issue was addressed by journalist and host Raúl Fitipaldi in an exclusive conversation with Jorge Majfud\*, writer, novelist, and professor at Jacksonville University, for* Portal Desacato, *transcribed below:*

**Raúl Fitipaldi:** *Does the United States have any legitimate claims regarding the administration of the Panama Canal?*

**Jorge Majfud.** None. Quite the opposite. They are obligated to pay multibillion-dollar compensation for the crimes committed in that country, from Theodore Roosevelt to George H. Bush and beyond. Of course, this is a moral obligation—meaning irrelevant.

The Canal was never the United States' property, nor were Americans the ones who built it. Roosevelt invented a revolution in that Colombian province when its congress rejected the offer to continue the project initiated under French direction because it would surrender sovereignty for a laughable sum (we examined this in *The Savage Frontier: 200 Years of Anglo-Saxon Fanaticism in Latin America*, 2021). As always, the solution was to intervene in a foreign country, invent a new nation, and then have the Panamanian "rebels" sign a treaty with a gun to their heads—as was and remains customary.

The Canal was built by 50,000 Caribbean laborers who were left out of the picture, working under conditions of slavery. Six thousand of them died during construction while Roosevelt called them lazy and stupid Negroes.

Washington will pay no compensation, just as it hasn't paid for all the dictatorships and massacres it carried out in Latin America and the rest of the world. On the contrary, it continues bullying others while playing the victim. The classic master of what was then called "the free race" (whites)—a thief and rapist who accused Blacks and mestizos of being thieves and rapists. The same happened when Haiti freed itself from France and slavery yet was forced to pay exorbitant compensation to imperial slaveholders for over a century. The same as the white masters in the U.S., who received compensation for losing their "private property"—not the enslaved people.

**RF.** *Does Panama have the necessary sovereignty to defend the Torrijos-Carter Treaties that returned the Canal to them?*

**JM.** No. In international relations, empires sign treaties until they no longer serve their interests. We've seen this repeatedly with treaties Washington signed with Indigenous peoples, with Mexicans, with Caribbean nations—from the 18th century to today, when in 2015 Obama signed the nuclear technology limitation treaty with Iran, only for Trump to renounce it the next day (two years later).

Now, concerning Mexico, Panama, Canada, Colombia, or Europe, we should remember the maxim of Henry Kissinger, one of its most celebrated criminals: *"Being an enemy of the United States is dangerous, but being its friend is lethal."*

Panama has only two options: (1) prostitute itself like one of Trump's lackeys to receive something in return, or (2) establish a state policy based on agreements and alliances with more reliable countries—those that share its security concerns regarding the eternal enforcement of the Monroe Doctrine. That is, commercial treaties and strategic unions with its Latin American siblings and other nations, whether European, African, or Asian.

This idea of the value of unity comes from Native North Americans: you can easily break a single spear, but try breaking several bundled together and you won't succeed. The Anglo-Saxon colonists listened and learned so quickly they didn't give Native nations time to unite effectively. Today, it's an ironic symbol on the U.S. coat of arms.

**RF.** *Is there any basis to Donald Trump's accusations that China is exploiting the Canal for itself?*

**JM:** It's false and contradictory. China's presence in Panama is negligible. The problem is that China keeps doing things right—and like any industrial and commercial power, it has the right to use the Panama Canal and any other port if it doesn't employ violence, as is traditional with the U.S. and Anglo-Saxon empires.

What bothers people most about China is that it has regained its status as a global superpower without invading or destroying any country. The "impoverishing communists" have not only outpaced others in development, but successful capitalists owe them fortunes.

If the United States were even moderately intelligent—reasonable instead of fanatical—it would manage its terrible economic, financial, and social problems and its imperial decline through a negotiated transition with China to secure strategic collaboration. But instead, Washington is desperately begging for a violent end to its hegemony.

In the U.S., we have everything needed to be a developed and happier country, but we're the exact opposite—despite still being a global superpower that can create the world's reserve currency by pressing zeros on a keyboard. What's supposed to happen when we no longer have those privileges and, on top of that, must face a world that won't forgive us for having been such sons of bitches for so long?

**RF.** *How should the affected countries in Latin America—both directly and indirectly, whether on the Pacific or Atlantic coasts—respond?*

**JM.** A reasonable short-term response would be "negotiate with Trump." It's more or less what Mexico just did to suspend tariffs for a month. We can partly understand Claudia Sheinbaum: her citizens come first, and she doesn't want a recession hitting the poorest, however brief.

The more strategic long-term response is simply to *not negotiate with an extortionist*. There's no need to even engage in a dialectical, media, or diplomatic dispute. *Silence and indifference are the only effective way to deal with a bully.*

If Trump imposes 25% tariffs, Mexico should impose 30%. Of course, this must be done in coordination with other affected parties like Canada, China, and Europe, and with future victims of the Alpha Male's new aggressions.

Mexico should seek to place its products in other markets. This wouldn't just teach a lesson about what happens when a country disrespects another, but also secure greater future stability.

Mexico is the United States' main trade partner and vice versa—but when has the U.S. ever treated Mexico as an equal or even with basic respect? Only the willfully blind don't see it.

Trump thinks he'll reverse his empire's decline by harassing smaller economies, but playing along only feeds the beast. It's harmful to the world and to us here in the U.S., where we must prolong the agony of a psychotic mindset that can't be happy even with all the world's gold.

# THere are THingS Money can'T Buy–and THaT's WHaT InfuriaTes THem MOST

When the U.S. kept slaves in chains, it presented itself as a democracy's exemplar. Even today, some insist it's never had a dictatorship.

South Africa's apartheid was defended by Ronald Reagan as a bastion of freedom on that "black-prone-to-socialism" continent, while Nelson Mandela remained on London and Washington's lists of "dangerous terrorists."

How can Israel—an apartheid regime by all international human rights organizations' accounts and by many Israelis' own admission—be called a democracy? A brutal regime, licensed to kill and massacre at will, armed with foreign billions in weapons and high-tech, then weeping as if it were the universal victim.

What decent mind can justify massacring tens of thousands of children while insisting those who survive—starved, traumatized, amputated—must die, and as if that weren't enough, being fawned over by the trembling (*quaking*) leaders of the world's right and left?

I've collected a trove of cowardly threats (*bans*, blacklists)—none scare me—but also the solidarity of countless decent Jews who refuse to be corrupted by that fanatical, racist, supremacist ideology.

I'll repeat it a thousand times. They can kill as many thousands as they want, can threaten the billions on this planet who protest this barbarity, but they'll never kill others' dignity—something these well-armed, applauded genocidal cowards never had.

History has a septic tank waiting for them just around the corner.

# JILL STEIN: "WE HAVE THE BEST DEMOCRACY MONEY CAN BUY"

*Jorge Majfud speaks with the U.S. Green Party's presidential candidate.*

*The Uruguayan writer and academic spoke on September 4th at Jacksonville University's Terry Concert Hall with America's third presidential hopeful. Criticism of local policy pillars: two-party system, immigration, economy, guns, foreign policy, alignment with Israel.*

**Jorge Majfud:** *Jill, thank you so much for accepting our invitation to Jacksonville University. I hadn't planned this, but we must start with very bad news. Just minutes ago we learned there was another school shooting. In Georgia, where four people died—two teachers and two students. This is an endless story that's somehow connected to our conversation today, for instance about lobbying. Would you like to briefly comment on this?*

**Jill Stein:** Yes, absolutely. The news of this latest shooting is devastating, both for the loss of human lives and because it involves a 14-year-old boy who perpetrated the shooting. It's one tragedy after another. And the fact that this is so routine. Every year there are so many mass shootings. Americans have conflicting feelings. Many want common-sense gun control.

The Second Amendment is here to stay, at least in the foreseeable future, but the American people want to see action and many support measures like banning assault weapons, a voluntary buyback program, waiting periods, raising the minimum age for purchases, ending open carry, red flag laws that apply when gun owners are in a highly dangerous situation and at risk of harming others or themselves. There are many things we could do to reduce gun violence within legal bounds.

Unfortunately, we're up against very powerful interests—in this case, the National Rifle Association. There are many other examples of powerful lobbying groups that essentially buy their way to act or, more commonly, to not act, to block the passage of laws that have broad public support. I'd add it's not just lobbyist power but the very essence of our political system that's bought and sold with vast sums of money.

Studies have shown that laws passed in the U.S. Congress are those backed by extremely powerful financial interests. There was a study from Northwestern and Princeton—maybe ten years ago, a definitive analysis of decades of policies—that demonstrated very clearly there's almost no correlation between public priorities and what Congress actually passes. So this great tragedy we're hearing about today, which is so commonplace and could be substantially reduced, is the rule rather than the exception regarding how laws get passed or blocked, and whom elected politicians serve.

I should add this is part of why the Green Party exists and why people like me run for public office outside the *Big Money* political system, so we can have policies that truly address the urgent needs and interests of the American people. Because we don't take corporate money, we don't use super *PACs* that let certain individuals pour unlimited millions—what's also called Dark Money. Similarly, there are many campaign funds, so-called "victory funds" (I think they started with Hillary Clinton's 2016 campaign), allowing a single donor to write a check up to a million dollars directly benefiting a presidential campaign, even though Federal Election Commission laws limit individual donations to $3,300 per election cycle. That's not small change, but it's peanuts compared to a million dollars—or more if you go the Super PAC route.

*We have the best democracy money can buy*, which is no democracy at all, explaining why politicians sell themselves right before our eyes and why it's routine for elected officials to take marching orders from big donors rather than earning the people's trust.

**JM:** *You mentioned the Second Amendment. The U.S. Constitution is so old it resembles a religious text, open to multiple interpretations. In the 1930s, the Supreme Court had a completely different interpretation of that amendment than today's. That shift stems basically from the NRA's lobbying beginning in the 1970s. Meaning it's fundamentally an interpretive issue. You wouldn't even need to amend the constitution to regulate these matters. In an airport, for example, the Second Amendment doesn't apply.*

*Now, Jill, what's the key difference in these aspects between the Twin Parties (Democrat and Republican), the establishment, and the Green Party? Beyond money...*

**JS:** Well, I think the main difference between the Green Party and the established parties is money. It's what pulls the strings in the big picture. On the other hand, the result of this is that Greens can advocate for meeting the truly urgent needs of ordinary people. We're not fighting for what the lobbies want, we're fighting for what the people want. What do I mean by this? I mean things like healthcare that should be a human right for all. We have an endless crisis in this country. Despite the passage of the *Affordable Care Act*, healthcare still isn't affordable—far from it.

About 60 million Americans don't have adequate healthcare—they're either uninsured or lack minimum adequate coverage. We could have a public system like expanded and improved Medicare for All that covers mental health, dental care, vision, hearing, and chronic illnesses... All this should be covered by Medicare for All. Currently, it isn't, unless millions of people want to spend every last dollar to get their insurance to cover these services. If you have chronic conditions, it's even harder. Right now, when someone gets a cancer diagnosis, there's over a 40 percent chance they'll spend their life savings within two years. They might even lose their home, just from treating their cancer.

That's why Greens advocate for healthcare for all as a human right. Plus, with Medicare for All, we'd save half a trillion dollars annually because having a single insurance provider instead of hundreds would save enormous amounts on bureaucracy. Right now, we need an entire army of bureaucrats just to determine which insurance company will cover you, whether they'll cover everything you need. If someone goes to a hospital and needs an aspirin, this bureaucracy checks whether their insurance covers aspirin and, if so, how many. I'm not exaggerating—it's with this kind of red tape that we're currently spending one out of every three healthcare dollars just on bureaucracy.

Medicare for All would eliminate all that and reduce overall costs from 30 percent to 3 percent. By cutting these administrative expenses, we could expand healthcare coverage and still have half a trillion dollars left over. So this is one of the Green Party's main issues.

Another is endless wars. Right now, half of every congressional dollar goes to the endless war machine. That amounts to about a trillion dollars per year. We advocate cutting that percentage by at least 50 percent. Currently, the U.S. spends more than the next ten arms buyers combined. What does all this get us? It gets us lots of military interventions.

According to the Congressional Research Service, over the past 30 years we've sent our military on 250 interventions. These are trillions of dollars we're spending on war after war that don't make the world safer—and don't make us safer either. We're getting involved in all kinds of conflicts we shouldn't be in, so that's another key difference. We advocate cutting the military budget, having a defensive rather than offensive policy, and redirecting those dollars toward real security here at home—toward better healthcare, better education.

I should also mention we fight for tuition-free public higher education as another Human Right. We had it in my day, when public higher education was free or nearly free. We demand relief for students facing virtually unpayable student loans. We demand these loans be paid as a crucial public investment to unleash our economy's incredible productivity. We know that for every dollar spent on higher education, seven dollars return to the economy.

I'm just mentioning some of the issues Greens focus on beyond our environmental policies. We're also sounding the alarm about the serious housing access crisis. We have a housing emergency in this country where half of all renters spend between 30 to 50 percent of their income on rent. People are in dire financial straits trying not to lose their homes. We demand federal rent control. We demand an end to the power of private capital, of powerful *private equity* firms, which can buy up homes and keep them vacant just to drive up costs and reduce housing supply. We also demand tenant rights regulations through executive order so they can't be evicted simply because the landlord wants to raise the rent at will. Additionally, we call for the construction of social housing. During the Clinton administration, a bill called the Faircloth Amendment was passed, which eliminated public funding for social housing construction.

Essentially, institutional public housing was gutted, allowing social housing to deteriorate over the following decades, so today there's very little public housing left, and what exists is of very poor quality.

Therefore, we demand reinvestment in public housing as a social good. Housing is a Human Right just like healthcare. We can't allow capital to exploit housing until it becomes completely unaffordable, creating the crisis we have today. We estimate that a reasonable investment would be 15 million units of quality, affordable public housing built according to comprehensive ecological principles— meaning they'd be highly energy efficient, include public transportation access to avoid contributing to current problems of urban sprawl, traffic pollution and congestion, etc. This way we'll also protect natural spaces through concentrated housing that includes green spaces as an essential component of healthy communities and dwellings. People are much healthier when they have access to green spaces and recreational areas.

**JM:** *We have a structural problem in our electoral system, which is highly indirect and based on a legacy of slavery. States like Texas, California and New York require twice as many votes as Alaska or Mississippi per elector, undermining the democratic principle of "one person, one vote." Additionally, each state, regardless of population, elects two senators, so sparsely populated states like Alaska, with less than a million inhabitants, have equal Senate representation as populous states like California, home to nearly 40 million people.*

*Currently, the real alternative party is the Abstention Party, with about 80 million eligible voters who didn't participate in the 2020 election. In that election, Biden received 81 million votes. Many feel their vote doesn't matter in so-called Blue States. For example, in California, Biden got 11 million votes compared to Trump's 6 million. Even if 3 to 5 million people voted for an alternative party, it wouldn't change the electoral distribution due to the "winner takes all" system.*

*How difficult do you see changing this old system to make it more democratic?*

**Stein:** Great point. How do we create a real democratic system? There are many aspects of our current system that are actually anti-democratic. This includes not just the Electoral College but also the first-past-the-post system that awards all electoral votes to whichever candidate gets the most popular votes—not necessarily a majority. It's the *Ballot Access Law* that makes it very difficult by design for other options to appear on the ballot. Currently people are starting to demand more choices. We see this in every poll that comes out. One conducted by Gallup asks people every year: Are you satisfied with the two-party system or do you see a need for another option? That number keeps rising each year. Currently, 63 percent of Americans say: "Yes, we really need another alternative political party because the two we have are doing a very poor job and aren't serving the public interest."

There are many factors contributing to the democracy crisis. The difficulty third parties face in getting on ballots is part of this crisis. Maybe you've seen recent news about our court battles for ballot access. We're fighting to provide another choice in these elections— a choice that's anti-war, against genocide, pro-worker, and that addresses the climate emergency, issues the traditional party campaigns aren't talking about.

We're fighting to get into the public debates organized by the major television networks. If we leave it solely to the two main players, they won't say a word about the genocide, about the endless war machine that's also robbing us blind, about the climate crisis. We don't hear them talking about that at all. The Democrats, in particular, claim they've solved the problem, but they're not solving it—and we can discuss this in more detail later. While they claim to be climate protection advocates, we know, for example, that both Joe Biden and Barack Obama broke all records for fossil fuel emissions and exports, making the U.S. the top fossil fuel producer. No. It doesn't work that way.

Actually, the climate doesn't care about renewable energy. The climate cares about fossil fuel production. The Democrats have handled this issue just as poorly as the Republicans. In fact, they've outperformed the Republicans, both in extraction from public lands and in selling off public lands specifically for fossil fuel exploitation. That's why we're fighting to be on the ballots—so people have an alternative.

Well, we were talking about our democracy crisis within the system, and one thing I haven't mentioned yet is the role of money in politics, which is completely out of control. Maybe you saw the Democratic Convention recently, the one covered by Chris Cuomo from *News Nation*…

**JM:** *Yes, I saw it. Cuomo mentioned the suites in the upper ring of the Chicago Bulls' stadium, which cost between $500,000 and $5 million each.*

**JS:** Each!

**JM:** *Those are the Democratic and Republican party donors. Meanwhile, Kamala Harris was talking about putting limits on the rich and taxing their profits. I suppose they were laughing…*

*Regarding alternative parties, the New York Times published a report today showing that in local U.S. elections, the majority of ballots had only one candidate—mostly Republicans—in states like Missouri. This also relates to plutocracy, which has impacted this country's democratic history.*

*The massive conglomerates created after the Civil War continued the legacy of slaveholding corporations. In 1888, Christian Rutherford Hayes complained: "The great problem is the immense wealth and power in the hands of a few. Hundreds of Congressional laws are passed in favor of these people and against the working class. This is no longer government of the people, by the people, and for the people, but government of the corporations, by the corporations, and for the corporations." This quote is from 1888.*

*According to a 2016 US Today investigation, thousands of laws (they mentioned over 10,000, with 2,000 passed) were "copy and paste" texts that congressmembers received from major corporations. Further proof of legalized corruption.*

*It's as if political democracy is trapped in an economic dictatorship. Under these conditions—due to the electoral system's structure and lack of funding—I see it as very difficult for an alternative party to change this reality.*

*How do you think change could be possible, from a practical standpoint?*

**JS:** Well, that's the million-dollar question. How can we change such a closed system? One proof of how hard it is to change anything in this system is that in March 2024, the Democratic Party announced they'd hired an army of lawyers to eliminate competitors like me from the ballots. They hire lawyers to wage legal warfare (*lawfare*) with technical closures, challenging the spirit of laws and finding small backdoors to eliminate competition. This is profoundly undemocratic behavior from start to finish. But they didn't stop there. They blocked us in three states, but failed because we fought them in court and won those lawsuits. Then they started posting job ads to recruit infiltrators and spies to hack our ballot access. They also hijacked the little public funding we were entitled to—that money candidates are supposed to have so they don't sell their souls to the highest bidder.

We were one of the few parties that actually used these funds. Now, for the past two months, they owe us about $300,000 of these funds, but they found a technical excuse not to release it. We'll probably receive it in the coming weeks, but their clear goal was to block it to make it even harder for us to stay in the electoral race. This is the Democratic Party.

Let me tell you something else. In 2022, they impersonated the Green Party and called many people who had signed a petition for one of our candidates running for federal office in the North Carolina Senate race. They called these people claiming to be the Green Party. They were Democratic infiltrators. They wanted people to withdraw their signatures because they didn't want our candidate to stay in the race. Fortunately, we recorded one of these calls, reported them, and the Democratic Party was found guilty. They didn't call it by its real name—fraudulent interference in an election. Because apparently it's not called election interference when a party impersonates another and fraudulently claims to represent them to eliminate certain candidates from the race.

So I just want to remind everyone (since people always talk about Republicans interfering in elections) that Democrats do it too, and they do it shamelessly before elections even begin. We don't need to wait for Donald Trump to bring fascism—fascism is already here.

Now, returning to your question. How can we solve this problem when they're in power and control the media? Well, fortunately their control isn't absolute. They don't control all social media. As you said, in 2020, one in three voters didn't vote because they weren't buying what the candidates were selling. In 2016, voter abstention was even higher—around 42 percent. This shows Americans aren't satisfied with the status quo and are looking for alternatives. The question is when we'll reach the point of no return, because right now people are suffering tremendous economic and racial disparities. An entire generation is barely surviving. Recent polls show that among young people under 25, half say they have no hope for the future. A quarter say they've considered self-harm within the next two weeks.

Clearly things aren't working when you have two major parties bought by the war machine, Wall Street, insurance companies, and Big Pharma. When they're the ones running the *show*, ordinary people don't factor into their calculations. And ordinary people have clearly reached their breaking point. Sixty percent of Americans live paycheck to paycheck—they're obviously not happy with this.

For many voters, the genocide in Palestine is a red line, and they say they won't vote for either party because of it. Now we're seeing growing interest from organized grassroots movements supporting the Green Party campaign, suggesting we may have already reached that point of no return. The genocide in Gaza is part of that massive military-industrial apparatus that's robbing us and depriving us here of even the most basic necessities.

Three days ago, a poll of Muslim voters showed me tied with Kamala Harris—meaning their votes are splitting between the two candidates. This is unprecedented and represents a massive drop in Democratic support. Arab and Muslim Americans take the genocide very seriously because they're closely connected to what's happening in the region. American voters in general are also outraged by the waste of our tax dollars on endless war machinery while we lack healthcare, housing, and quality education here—things that much poorer countries have solved better than we have.

So I just want to emphasize that ours is a work in progress. Quoting Frederick Douglass: "Power concedes nothing without a demand." If we don't fight for our rights, we'll never get them. People can't be intimidated out of voting for what they want—whether it's peace in Palestine or slashing the military budget to fund education. People have always heard, "don't vote for what you need; vote where the power is." The question is whether we can break free from this once and for all.

Alice Walker once said that the surest way to lose power is to think we don't have any. But if you add up all the people who want to end the genocide in Palestine right now, or all those burdened by crushing student debt (44 million total), or the approximately 60 million without adequate health insurance—just these groups alone would form a voting bloc large enough to win a presidential election.

So in my view, the answer to your question about how we can break this system is that we need courage, conviction, and to reprogram the mental conditioning telling us we're powerless. That's always been their narrative, but we can rebel by recognizing our real power to enforce our demands through our votes—whether at 5% or 51%. We must start building our path from where we stand without being intimidated. In a democracy, power resides in our votes, and by not exercising them, we'd be contributing to democracy's abolition.

**JM**: *Many await the return of a new 1960s (with its anti-war, anti-colonial and civil rights courage), but over the past 20 years we've instead slid toward a new Middle Ages. Now, from an even more reactionary standpoint—especially in the Republican Party with Trump and J.D. Vance—many seem ready to overturn democratic beliefs like equality or Enlightenment ideals. Many conservatives argue we must move toward a*

*Dark Enlightenment that eliminates our equal freedom of expression and education itself.*

*In June 2021, General Mark Milley testified before Congress about critical race theory and accusations of being Woke: "I've read Mao Zedong. I've read Karl Marx. I've read Lenin. That doesn't make me a communist."*

*In 2021-22, just 11 people filed 60% of thousands of book challenges. Thousands of books were removed from schools and libraries. Even concepts or words like homosexuality or slavery have been restricted, when not outright silenced. For freedom, the most devastating effect isn't just censorship, but self-censorship.*

*On August 2, Rey Rodrigues (Chancellor of Florida's State University System Board of Governors) emailed all Florida public colleges to "review relevant course materials, including textbooks... for antisemitic and/or anti-Israel bias."*

*Gonsales wrote: "Any course containing these keywords: Israel, Israeli, Palestine, Palestinian, Middle East, Zionism, Zionist, Judaism, Jew or Jews will be flagged for review." Some individuals and parties win elections chanting freedom, freedom, freedom—only to practice prohibition, prohibition, censorship once in power.*

*Jill, why this open assault on academic freedom? Are we finally transitioning from rendering free speech irrelevant (as during slavery) to directly censoring it—in freedom's name?*

**JS:** That's an excellent question. There's absolutely an attack on our academic freedom through book bans and idea suppression. The statistics are staggering—you mention 11 people censoring 60% of challenged books in America. That's unacceptable, undemocratic. Books and ideas are being erased... Remember Julian Assange's case and what it signified. Remember all assaults on free speech and protest like those on university campuses here and worldwide. There's political speech censorship too. Here in Tampa, a suburban movement was accused of being "foreign agents"—just a leftist group criticizing U.S. foreign policy. Those activists face 15-year prison threats for their views. I've experienced this too. In 2016, as an anti-war candidate opposing nuclear weapons, I was smeared as a "Russian agent." This smear conveniently served Hillary Clinton and Democrats wanting me gone. The Intelligence Committee investigated me for three years—forcing me to prove my innocence, which is absurd. No one should have to prove their innocence. The burden of proof is on them to show you're guilty.

**JM**: A new McCarthyism...

**JS**: Exactly. A new kind of McCarthyism, like what's happening today, for example in the Democratic Party, which tries to stop its opponents this way. This is what democracy has become. That's why I insist we shouldn't wait for Trump to win to see fascism take root in this country. We already have our local police forces being trained by Israeli defense forces across the nation, learning abusive tactics. Currently, there are about 80 cities like Atlanta where police receive this training. Conscription has also returned. If you have children between 18 and 25, Uncle Sam's databases know exactly where they are. We live in a heavily militarized society, and the price we pay is our democracy, our right to protest, and our freedom of speech.

The reason Julian Assange was persecuted was for exposing war crimes, abuses, corruption, and torture. That's the role of journalism. Journalism shouldn't be the watchdog of power. That's why we're in the electoral race, in debates, discussions, and media. Because the foundations of our democracy, our economy, our environment are being auctioned off behind our backs to the highest bidder.

We're ruled by a plutocracy, by the very few who are extremely wealthy, because our political system has been privatized, and thus wealth grows increasingly concentrated. The three richest people in the United States have more money than the bottom 50% of the population.

To quote the late Supreme Court Justice Louis Brandeis: "We must choose between a large concentration of wealth and democracy" - we can't have both, and unfortunately we've chosen wealth concentration. Hence this legalized corruption. Now when will we have a real discussion about this? That won't happen with the two political parties staging this spectacle. They won't allow more voices or parties so people can fight for their own causes.

**JM**: *Jill, let's talk briefly about Latin America before addressing U.S. immigration issues.*

*After the United States seized over half of Mexican territory—from Texas to California—to expand slavery where it was previously illegal, the expansion stopped at the Rio Grande. This was to avoid incorporating areas densely populated by what congressmen of the time considered "inferior races." Instead, the U.S. established protectorates and military bases across Latin America.*

*In the 19th century, Washington carried out thousands of military interventions in Latin America to "teach Blacks how to govern themselves." This continued into the 20th century.*

*During the Great Depression, the U.S. withdrew marines from some "banana republics" but left their homegrown psychopaths in power—dictatorships that lasted generations.*

*During World War II, Washington neglected Latin America, allowing the region to regain about a dozen democracies. But the newly born CIA simply replaced the word "Blacks" with "communists" in all its rhetoric.*

*Once again, Washington sent tidal waves of dollars to fund armies and coups across Latin America.*

*In 1959, Senator John F. Kennedy told Congress: "I don't believe giving this aid to South America strengthens them against the Soviet Union... It's money down the drain militarily, but politically we hope they'll use it effectively."*

*President Nixon confirmed this approach in 1970: "I'll never agree with policies weakening Latin American militaries. They're power centers subject to our influence. The others [intellectuals] aren't."*

*By the 1970s, a dozen Latin American democracies had been lost, transformed into bloody military dictatorships (or "compliant democracies"), guardians of "free enterprise" for U.S. corporations and their accomplices—the Latin American oligarchy.*

*This history never ended; today it continues through other means.*

*Jill, considering this long history, what would Green Party foreign policy look like?*

**JS:** Without doubt our policy would be radically different. Since World War II, the CIA has carried out over 75 covert operations aimed at regime change, like in Guatemala to block land reform, against the interests of the United Fruit Company which held a monopoly while peasants starved. Simultaneously, Britain and the CIA prevented Iran's government from nationalizing its oil. So they overthrew democratically elected President Mohammad Mosaddegh and installed the Shah, a brutal dictator who remained for decades until the Islamic Revolution toppled him.

When the United States conducts these interventions, it not only causes immense harm in those countries but also creates blowback here at home. Due to global instability, failed states emerge like Libya—where open-air slave markets appeared after U.S. and NATO interventions overthrew and murdered Gaddafi. Soon after, we see mass migrations of millions from these nations.

The Green Party wants to replace this militaristic neocolonial intervention model with a human rights-based policy. Instead of envisioning a world dominated by American empire, we'd work toward a multipolar community of nations where international law prevails.

The United States is no longer the dominant power. We can't keep behaving like the schoolyard bully *harassing* others. This unipolar world benefits no one. Currently we face three extremely dangerous flashpoints—two active military conflicts (Ukraine and Israel) plus the threat of war with China potentially leading to nuclear confrontation. We're all endangered by this toxic imperial dominance mindset and must move beyond it.

**JM**: *Undocumented immigrants have significantly lower crime rates than U.S. citizens despite having a disproportionate number of young males. Yet whenever one commits a crime, it immediately makes headlines and politicians escalate criminalization of an entire disenfranchised group with no congressional lobby.*

*They don't know the language or laws, yet still manage to find jobs crucial to our society. Unlike corporate-outsourced labor abroad, they produce and consume here—ready to work immediately without 12-20 years of government-funded education and healthcare investments.*

*We oppose illegal immigration but also oppose criminalizing an extremely vulnerable population. Typically, desperate impoverished people take $10,000-$15,000 loans from coyotes to come here illegally. Why? Because U.S. immigration laws despise poor workers. At a U.S. embassy, you're better off claiming to be a lazy person with an impressive bank account than a hard worker if you want visa approval. Proportionally, the U.S. ranks among the world's least welcoming nations for refugees.*

*What would the Green Party's immigration policy look like?*

The most important step is stopping the crises we create through foreign interventions. We must respect other nations' sovereignty. We'd treat drug abuse as a public health issue rather than criminal matter—starting with marijuana legalization and studying decriminalization of other drugs to weaken cartels. We'd implement economic policies helping other nations so people don't need to emigrate. Remember we've overthrown two Haitian governments, slashing minimum wages and forcing mass emigration.

We'd also lift illegal economic sanctions against Cuba, Venezuela and Nicaragua—sanctions that forcibly displace populations. At the Mexican border, instead of walls we'd implement efficient identification systems to screen criminals while providing work permits. The vast majority of immigrants are honest, peaceful people. Most drug smuggling involves Americans—not migrants. Immigrants represent tremendous economic potential, projected to contribute $7 trillion to this economy next decade.

**JM:** *Trump stated that "if someone wants to eliminate Israel, then we don't want them in our country." On August 15, Trump blamed "our leftist media institutions" for the rise in antisemitism.*

*Antisemitism, historically associated with far-right groups, has been increasing due to a neo-Nazi resurgence in both Europe and the United States, even before the recent conflict in Gaza.*

*Trump also blamed "a certain candidate for president of the United States, which is hard to believe in our universities..." I think he was talking about you. Who else? Certainly not Mrs. Harris. How do you respond to these easy, common accusations that conflate Zionism and Judaism? What can you tell us about IPAC, the Zionist lobby?*

A very common mistake is confusing Judaism with Zionism. Zionism is a political ideology, not a religion. I grew up in a Jewish community, attended a synagogue where everyone understood that Jews had suffered a Holocaust and that this should never happen to anyone again. In that community, we were clear that those who looked the other way and allowed it were also guilty. This is not a religious conflict - in what is now Palestine, Muslims, Jews and Christians lived in peace until the Zionists arrived and began having problems not only with Palestinians but with Muslims and Christians alike.

Until the 1990s, access to Israel's national archives wasn't permitted, and only then did we learn more clearly what happened before Israel's founding. Zionism sought to take land where other people already lived through ethnic cleansing. Having been victims of genocide doesn't entitle them to commit genocide themselves.

The genocide must stop. The separatist state of Israel must withdraw from Gaza and the West Bank - currently also in the process of being occupied. Israel's ethnic cleansing and apartheid must also end. This story didn't begin on October 7 but years before Israel's founding 77 years ago. International law must be upheld. This is demanded by the international community, the International Criminal Court and the United Nations. Looking the other way means endorsing torture and murder of men, women and children on an industrial scale.

According to Reuters polls, 68 percent of Americans want an immediate end to the genocide - and that's not antisemitism. To claim that demanding an end to genocide is antisemitic is itself a form of antisemitism. Opposing genocide represents one of the highest principles not just of Judaism, Christianity and Islam, but of humanity itself.

This slaughter must stop. It could end with a simple phone call like Reagan made regarding Lebanon, where hundreds of thousands were saved from massacre during the pursuit of the Palestine Liberation Organization - somewhat like Hamas at the time. Israeli Prime Minister Menachem Begin had to stop bombing Lebanon and withdraw troops. Eisenhower did the same when Israel invaded Egypt, and now we must do the same to force Netanyahu - a war criminal - to comply. If he doesn't, weapons supplies should be cut off. Yet more weapons are being provided, contrary to U.S. laws prohibiting arms to human rights violators who block humanitarian aid - including those not complying with nuclear arms control treaties, as Israel isn't a signatory to the Nuclear Non-Proliferation Treaty. That's why U.S. aid to Israel is illegal and should end immediately.

We would enforce the law on our first day in government to stop this tragedy. Israel must comply with international law, and we have the power to stop it. A fascist state isn't compatible with international law. We can't normalize the industrial-scale torture and murder of children.

We're all threatened by this war machinery existing worldwide, which should start by halting the genocide in Gaza right now. On the other hand, we must reduce the global arms race. No one is safe in this world. We're all implicated and impoverished by this war machine.

www.ingramcontent.com/pod-product-compliance
Lightning Source LLC
Chambersburg PA
CBHW022005090426

42741CB00007B/900